The Last Days

A Study of the Book of Revelation

The Last Days

A Study of the Book of Revelation

E A Adeboye

Published by RoperPenberthy Publishing Ltd
Springfield House, 23 Oatlands Drive, Weybridge, Surrey KT13 9LZ

Text copyright © E A Adeboye, 2010

All Bible quotations are from the Authorised (King James) Version of the Holy Bible.

This Edition published 2010
First published August 1994
Reprint January 2009
Reprinted 2015

ISBN 978 1 903905 62 3

All rights reserved. No portion of this publication may be translated into any language or reproduced in any form except for brief quotations in reviews, without prior written permission of the author.

Initially published by Christ the Redeemer's Ministries
Contact Address:
Redeemed Christian Church of God, Central Office UK, Redemption House, Station Road,
Knebworth, Hertfordshire SG3 6AT United Kingdom

Cover design by Audri Coleman

Typeset by Avocet Typeset, Chilton, Aylesbury, Buckinghamshire

Introduction

The Book of Revelation is divided into sections. Chapter 1 describes to us the glory of the risen Christ. Chapters 2 and 3 contain letters to the churches. Chapters 4 and 5 tell us what will be going on in Heaven after the church has been raptured, while chapters 6 to 19 tell us what will happen to those who are left behind.

Chapter 20 tells us what will happen to the devil when he is imprisoned, that the books of life will be opened and a judgement will take place of those who are fit to enter the Kingdom and those who will go into the lake of fire. Finally, in chapters 21 and 22 we read about the new earth and a new Heaven.

It is an open secret that many born-again Christians ignore reading the Book of Revelation. There are a number of reason for this. First and foremost is the fact that only a few people understand the coded messages in the book. Few scholars have been able to decode the messages in the book. There have also been various schools of thought on the codes. Those who understand only part of it are scared of the last days.

Also, there have been few books and commentaries on the study of the Book of Revelation. THE LAST DAYS, no doubt, will successfully fill a gap in the lack of study books on the Book of Revelation. The author has taken great pains to decode all the messages, in some instances, verse by verse. This will be a good reference point both for theological students and for Christians in general.

Preface

The second coming of Jesus Christ will definitely take place is very soon. We do not know when He will come again, but recent events in the world, juxtaposed with what is revealed to us in the Book of Revelation, point to the fact that He will come very soon.

God is also almost ready for the second coming of Jesus Christ. Christians should hold fast because the day of redemption draws near. We should hold fast to what we have so that no one will take our crown.

If you overcome, Jesus Christ will give you Himself. If you do not overcome, you will be around when trouble starts. On the day of judgement, we will all stand before God individually. We will be judged individually. We will be rewarded individually.

The only way out of the trouble that is coming is to receive the mark of Jesus Christ. His grace will be more than sufficient to take you through the last days.

Pastor E. A. Adeboye

Table of Contents

Introduction		v
Preface		vii
Chapter 1	All Will Be Well	1
Chapter 2	The Revelation of Jesus Christ	7
Chapter 3	Jesus Will Return With The Saints	14
Chapter 4	The Vision of The Glorified Christ	19
Chapter 5	Letters to the Churches – The Church in Ephesus	26
Chapter 6	The Letter to The Church In Smyrna	34
Chapter 7	The Letter to The Church In Pergamos	40
Chapter 8	The Letter to The Church In Thyatira	45
Chapter 9	The Letter to The Church In Sardis	50
Chapter 10	The Letter to The Church in Philadelphia	56
Chapter 11	The Letter to The Church of the Laodicea	62
Chapter 12	The Door Of Heavenly Revelation	68
Chapter 13	Jesus Christ is the Lamb And the Lion	74
Chapter 14	Israel's Missing Week	81
Chapter 15	The Tribulation Saints	89

Chapter 16	God is the Controller of the Weather	94
Chapter 17	Sealing of the Tribulation Saints	98
Chapter 18	Salvation is from GOD alone	108
Chapter 19	The Judgement of the Trumpets	118
Chapter 20	The Joys and Sorrows of a prophet	129
Chapter 21	The Antichrist	133
Chapter 22	The True Temples of Christ	137
Chapter 23	The Two Witnesses	141
Chapter 24	The Woman and the Child	151
Chapter 25	The Antichrist is the Beast	159
Chapter 26	The Christian is the one…	167
Chapter 27	The Song of Moses and the Lamb	178
Chapter 28	The Wrath of God	184
Chapter 29	The Babylonian Cult	194
Chapter 30	The Fall of Babylon	196
Chapter 31	The Marriage of the Lamb	207
Chapter 32	Christians are Winners	214
Chapter 33	The Honeymoon	220
Chapter 34	The Judgement of the Great White Throne	230
Chapter 35	The New Heaven and the New Earth	237
Chapter 36	The New Jerusalem	244
Chapter 37	Surely I Come Quickly	250

Chapter 1

ALL WILL BE WELL

The Book of Revelation is a very important book, but it is also the most difficult book to understand in the Bible. This is because what God wrote there is in a code language. Unless you understand this code, you will not understand the book.

What is written in the Book of Revelation is meant for those who love God. If everybody will understand its contents, they will be saved. They will cry for salvation. It is written that many are called but few are chosen (Matthew 22:14) and the reason some people will not be chosen is that they have eyes but they cannot see. Also, they have ears but they cannot hear.

Apart from the letters to the churches, the message of the Book of Revelation is basically in two parts. Firstly, the book is saying that all will be well with us. Secondly, it is saying it will get worse before it gets better. The book talks about the age to come as well as the age that is passing away. The age to come will be one of marvellous blessings but before this, the present age that must give birth to the next one. There must be a period that can best be described as a period of labour pains.

A time of rejoicing will come. There will be much dancing and many blessings, but between now and then there will be a period of labour pains. The world and the universe are pregnant now. Very soon, they will deliver. When they deliver, all will be well.

In the age to come – the Messianic age when Jesus will reign for a thousand years – all will surely be well. Let us now discuss the blessings of the age.

A. THE WORLD WILL BECOME VERY FERTILE

All barren land will become fertile. Bible scholars tell us that during this period, every tree that is now not producing enough will be producing abundantly. Isaiah 51:3 says:

> *For the LORD shall comfort Zion: he will comfort all her waste places; and he will make her wilderness* like Eden, and her desert like the garden of the LORD; joy and gladness shall be found therein, thanksgiving, and the voice of melody.*

In other words, all those places we call desert will become like the Garden of Eden. Once upon a time, before man fell and the land became cursed, the land always produced bountifully. It was the fall of man that led to a curse being pronounced on the earth. This curse is recorded in Genesis 3:17-18.

People are eating potatoes today and rejoicing, not knowing that they are eating thorns. Originally, God did not even want us to eat vegetables. Vegetables are food for animals. He said that we were to eat fruit. Then we went against Him. He then made us to eat like animals. When the Lord returns, the curse shall be removed and we shall go back to our original diet. The animals will eat their food and we will go back to a diet of fruit.

B. ALL WARS WILL CEASE

There will be no more wars during the messianic age. In Isaiah 2:4, the Bible tells us what will happen when the Lord comes:

"And he shall judge among the nations, and shall rebuke many people: and they shall beat their swords into plowshares and their spears into pruninghooks: nation shall not lift up sword against nation, neither shall they learn war any more."

C. THERE WILL BE NO MORE ENMITY BETWEEN MAN AND BEAST

In the world to come, there will be no enmity between man and beast There will also be no enmity between beast and beast. Before man sinned in the Garden of Eden, all animals were friends; man and animals were living together in peace. As soon as the curse was pronounced on man, trouble started. In fact, it was after the curse that God said man should begin to eat meat. Before this time, we were only eating fruit.

No animal was killed before man sinned but as soon as sin entered in, God had to kill an animal in order to get skin to make a covering for us. From then till now, animals are being killed for no just cause. This curse will be removed in the new world.

Both the relationship between man and beast and the relationship between beast and beast in the world to come are highlighted in Isaiah 11:6-9:

"The wolf also shall dwell with the lamb, and the leopard shall lie down with the kid; and the calf and the young lion and the fatling together; and a little child shall lead them. And the cow and the bear shall feed; their young ones shall lie down together: and the lion shall eat straw like the ox. And the sucking child shall play on the hole of the asp, and the weaned child shall put his hand on the cockatrice' den. They shall not

hurt nor destroy in all my holy mountain: for the earth shall be full of the knowledge of the LORD, as the waters cover the sea."

D. THERE WILL BE NO MORE WEARINESS, SORROW AND PAIN

Jeremiah 31:12:

Therefore they shall come and sing in the height of Zion, and shall flow together to the goodness of the LORD, for wheat, and for wine, and for oil, and for the young of the flock and of the herd: and their soul shall be as a watered garden; and they shall not sorrow any more at all.

Isaiah 35:10:

And the ransomed of the LORD shall return, and come to Zion with songs and everlasting joy upon their heads: they shall obtain joy. and gladness, and sorrow and sighing shall flee away.

There will be no sorrow because we will not die. All of us who will come back with Jesus Christ will put on glorious bodies so it will be impossible for us to die. We will be here just to enjoy life for a thousand years before we finally go back. We will meet some people on earth when we come back. During the seven years of tribulation, some people will have died. It is those who remain that we will meet. For those of us gloriously endowed, there will be no sicknesses or death.

Those who are not gloriously endowed will, however, fall ill. The Bible tells us that the leaves of some trees that will be growing at that time will be for the healing of the nations (Revelation 22:2). When those who are not yet transformed fall ill, they will pluck leaves from these trees and eat to get well.

Also, those not gloriously endowed will die, but not until they have reached the age of a hundred years (Isaiah 65:20-22). When they die, they will still be accursed.

In Isaiah 25:8, the Bible tells us:

He will swallow up death in victory; and the Lord GOD will wipe away tears from off all faces; and the rebuke of his people shall he take away from off all the earth: for the LORD hath spoken it.

At that time, there will be no more weeping, although however, those of us who get to Heaven will weep for joy. Also, when God begins, to reward us for what we have done on earth, we will weep. When you compare your reward to that of others and yours is smaller, you are likely to weep. However, God will say to you that there is no more need to weep.

E. IT WILL BE WORSE BEFORE GETTING BETTER

When Jesus was asked about the signs of His coming, He said a great deal. In Matthew 24:8, He said, "All these are the beginning of sorrows." In the original Greek, the word 'sorrow' means, 'the beginning of labour pains.' In Zephaniah 1:14, we are told that the great day of the Lord is near and mighty men shall cry bitterly. Those who are left behind after the rapture, no matter who they are, will cry. Even the mighty men will cry bitterly because of the pain that will come at that time. Joel 2:1 also confirms that at the day of the Lord, the whole world will tremble. Those who are left behind will suffer.

The Bible tells us that when this present age is to give birth to the next one, everything will be affected, including the sun, the moon and the stars. This is recorded in Joel 2:30-3l:

And I will shew wonders in the heavens and in the earth, blood, and fire, and pillars of smoke. The sun shall be turned into darkness, and the moon into blood, before the great and the terrible day of the LORD come.

The pains in the world will be so great that people will be fighting each other. You do not joke with someone who is in pain. It is going to be a terrible time and also a time of judgement. God is going to turn the whole world upside down and make it pass through fire (Malachi 3:1-3).

A sinner who does not repent and thinks that things are already tough, does not know what is coming; it is going to get worse. Christians will not be part of the labour pains because Jesus is going to take us away before the trouble starts. We shall not go through the tribulations, as some people believe. Matthew 24:36-42 gives a vivid description:

> *But of that day and hour knoweth no man, no, not the angels of heaven, but my Father only, But as the days of Noah were, so shall also the coming of the Son of man be. For as in the days that were before the flood they were eating and drinking, marrying and giving in marriage, until the day that Noah entered into the ark, And knew not until the flood came, and took them all away; so shall also the coming of the Son of man be. Then shall two be in the field; the one shall be taken, and the other left. Two women shall be grinding at the mill; the one shall be taken, and the other left, Watch therefore: for ye know not what hour your Lord doth come.*

It will be like in the days of Noah. Not a single drop of rain fell until Noah entered the ark. The ark of our own salvation is Jesus Christ. He will take us away before trouble starts.

The One who is going to open the door into the ark of salvation is Jesus Christ. He cannot be deceived. He knows whether you are a Christian or not. When the time comes to enter the ark of salvation, He will do the separation. He will send you back if you are not worthy. He knows you and He holds the key.

Chapter 2

THE REVELATION OF JESUS

Revelation 1:1-16:

The Revelation of Jesus Christ, which God gave unto him, to show unto his servants things which must shortly come to pass; and he sent and signified it by his angel unto his servant John: Who bare record of the word of God, and of the testimony of Jesus Christ, and of all things that he saw. Blessed is he that readeth, and they that hear the words of this prophecy, and keep those things, which are written therein: for the time is at hand. John to the seven churches which are in Asia: Grace be unto you, and peace, from him which is, and which was, and which is to come; and from the seven Spirits which are before his throne; And from Jesus Christ, who is the faithful witness, and the first begotten of the dead, and the prince of the kings of the earth. Unto him that loved us, and washed us from our sins in his own blood, And hath made us kings and priests unto God and his Father; to him be glory and dominion for ever and ever. Amen. Behold, he cometh with clouds; and every eye shall see him, and they also which pierced him: and all kindreds of the earth shall wail because of him. Even so, Amen. I am Alpha and Omega, the beginning and the ending, saith the Lord, which is, and which was, and which is to come, the Almighty. I John, who also am your brother, and companion in tribulation, and in the kingdom and patience of Jesus Christ, was in the isle that is called Patmos, for the word of God, and for the testimony of Jesus Christ. I was in the Spirit on the Lord's day, and heard behind me a great voice, as of a trumpet, Saying, I am Alpha and Omega, the first and the last: and, What thou seest, write in a book, and send it unto the seven churches which are in Asia; unto Ephesus, and unto Smyrna, and unto Pergamos, and unto Thyatira, and unto Sardis, and unto Philadelphia, and unto Laodicea. And I turned to see the voice that spake with me. And being turned, I saw seven golden candlesticks; And in the midst of the seven candlesticks one like unto the Son of man, clothed with a garment down to the foot, and girt about the paps with a golden girdle. His head and his hairs were white like wool, as white as snow; and his eyes were as a flame of fire; And his feet like unto fine brass, as if they burned in a furnace; and his voice as the sound of many waters. And he had in his right hand seven stars: and out of his mouth went a sharp two-edged sword: and his countenance was as the sun shineth in his strength.

The Book of Revelation contains the revelation of Jesus Christ that God, His Father, gave to Him. One would have thought that Jesus knew everything. However, when He was on earth, He said only His Father knew when He was coming back.

After Jesus rose from the dead and ascended to Heaven, the Father gave Him a Name that is above every other name. Everything that had been hidden was then revealed to Him. This implies that there are things that we do not know in this world that we shall know when we get to Heaven. This is why we should not judge God foolishly. Things that we do not comprehend on earth will be revealed to us when we get to Heaven.

The Book of Revelation shows us things that must surely come to pass very soon. Some people have said the book should not even be in the Bible. However, it is the most exciting book in the Bible and we have a lot to learn from it.

God sent the revelation to John through an angel (Rev. 22:16). Some people have said that when John saw this revelation, he was drunk. Some say he just had a dream. However, Jesus said that He sent His angel to inform John of these things. John gave us the report of everything he saw and heard. He was a good reporter, for in 1 John 1:1-13, he said:

That which was from the beginning, which we have heard, which we have seen with our eyes, which we have looked upon, and our hands have handled, of the Word of life; (For the life was manifested, and we have seen it, and bear witness, and shew unto you that eternal life, which was with the Father, and was manifested unto us;) That which we have seen and heard declare we unto you, that ye also may have fellowship with us: and truly our fellowship is with the Father, and with his Son Jesus Christ.

This means that everything he wrote down are things he saw, heard or touched. They are correct and not second-hand information.

John went further to say in Revelation 1:3 that *"blessed is he that reads and hears the words of this prophecy, and keep those things which are written therein, for the time is at hand"*. The Book of Revelation is full of blessings. There are seven places where the word *"blessed"*, is used. He said, *"Blessed are those who will read this book, hear its words and begin to plan their life accordingly"*.

In Revelation 14:13, John said, *"blessed are the dead who die in the Lord"*. If you are faithful and you serve Jesus Christ till you die, the Bible says you are blessed. John went on to say in Revelation 16:15 that if you are constantly watching and waiting for the second coming of Jesus Christ, you are blessed.

Let us look at Revelation 19:7-9:

> *Let us be glad and rejoice, and give honour to him: for the marriage of the Lamb is come, and his wife hath made herself ready. And to her was granted that she should be arrayed in fine linen, clean and white: for the fine linen is the righteousness of saints. And he saith unto me, Write, Blessed are they which are called unto the marriage supper of the Lamb. And he saith unto me, These are the true sayings of God.*

Those people who will be invited to the marriage of Jesus Christ are blessed. If the guests are blessed people, then, what about the bride herself? You may be wondering whether you will be invited to the marriage of the Lamb. You are the one who is to be married so you need no invitation. It will be your day of glory. The passage tells us that the bride has made herself ready rather than that the groom has made himself ready. It is my prayer that you will make yourself ready.

John said in Revelation 20:6:

Blessed and holy is he that hath part in the first resurrection: on such the second death hath no power, but they shall be priests of God and of Christ, and shall reign with him a thousand years.

The word "rapture" is not in the Bible. The phrase the Bible uses is, 'the first resurrection'. When Jesus comes again, He will come with His saints – that is, those who have already slept in the Lord and whose souls and spirits are in paradise. These saints will come down to earth to pick up their bodies. Jesus Christ will be waiting for them, in the air. After the saints have joined Him, those of us who are alive will go and meet them with our bodies already changed. This is the first resurrection, which is also called the rapture. Those of us who are part of this resurrection will never die again.

Revelation 22:7 says:

> *Blessed is he that keepeth the sayings of the prophecy of this book.*

When you have learnt the whole prophecy in this book, you keep it jealously and you let it guide your behaviour, you are blessed. Revelation 22:14 also says:

Blessed are they that do his commandments, that they may have right to the tree of life, and may enter in through the gates into the city.

Those who keep the commandments of God are blessed people. As a matter of fact, there is a tree that God planted in the Garden of Eden from which He never allowed Adam and Eve to eat. When we get to Heaven, we will be welcomed with fruit from this tree.

Revelation 1:4-5:

John to the seven churches which are in Asia: Grace be unto you, and peace, from him which is, and which was, and which is to come; and from the seven Spirits which are before his throne; And from Jesus Christ, who is the faithful witness, and the first begotten of the dead, and the prince of the kings of the earth. Unto him that loved us, and washed us from our sins in his own blood,

The Book of Revelation brought greetings from the Lord Almighty to the seven churches in Asia and to us. Some think that the book has nothing to do with us but 2 Timothy 3:16-17 says that all scriptures are given to every man by inspiration of God, that the man of God may be perfect, thoroughly furnished to all good works. The greetings in the book are given to all of us. The greetings are from the Father, the Holy Spirit and Jesus Christ. When it came to Jesus, "our Husband", we are told about Him in detail. Jesus is the faithful witness.

Let us look at Hebrews 1:1-2

God, who at sundry times and in divers manners spake in time past unto the fathers by the prophets, Hath in these last days spoken unto us by his Son, whom he hath appointed heir of all things, by whom also he made the worlds;

All those who had spoken in the past spoke about things that they heard from God. They relayed what God said to them. In the case of Jesus Christ, however, He said, "Verily, verily I say unto you" because He is the Lord. Jesus is the first begotten of the dead. Romans 8:29 explains this:

For whom he did foreknow, he also did predestinate to be confirmed to the image of his Son, that he might be the firstborn among many brethren.

If there is a first born then that means there is a second born, third born and so on. If the Bible had said Jesus is the only begotten from the dead, there would have been no hope for any of us of becoming children of God. Jesus is our elder brother. We are the children of God. When we get to Heaven, we will know the reality and glory of what this means.

Apart from being the first begotten of the dead, Jesus is also the Prince of the kings of the earth, according to Revelation 1:5. This means that He is the ruler of them all. Psalm 89:27 reveals to us that Jesus is higher than all the kings of the earth, but Revelation 1:6 tells us more:

And hath made us kings and priests unto God and his Father; to him be glory and dominion for ever and ever. Amen.

We are given three reasons why we must constantly glorify the name of Jesus Christ. First, because He loves us. This is enough for us. Romans 8:37 says we are more than conquerors because Jesus loves us. Second, because He washed us from our sins in His own blood. Each time you think about this, combine it with what the scriptures say in 1 John 1:7 that the blood of Jesus cleanses from all sins. Third, because He has made us kings and priests to God. This means that He recreated us. We used to be sinners, slaves, dogs and pagans but by the blood of Jesus Christ and the special grace of the Almighty God, we are now kings and priests.

Ephesians 2:11-14 assures us:

Wherefore remember, that ye being in time past Gentiles in the flesh, who are called Uncircumcision by that which is called the Circumcision in the flesh made by hands; that at that time ye were without Christ, being aliens from the commonwealth of Israel, and strangers from the covenants of promise, having no hope, and without God in the world: but now in Christ Jesus ye who sometimes were far off are made nigh by the blood of Christ. For he is our peace, who hath made both one, and hath broken down the middle wall of partition between us.

Even at the present time, God is our Father and so we have hope. To Him be glory and dominion forever and ever.

Chapter 3

JESUS WILL RETURN WITH THE SAINTS

Revelation 1:7-11:

> *Behold, he cometh with clouds; and every eye shall see him, and they also which pierced him: and all kindreds of the earth shall wail because of him. Even so, Amen. I am Alpha and Omega, the beginning and the ending, saith the Lord, which is, and which was, and which is to come, the Almighty. I John, who also am your brother, and companion in tribulation, and in the kingdom and patience of Jesus Christ, was in the isle that is called Patmos for the word of God, and for the testimony of Jesus Christ. I was in the Spirit on the Lord's day, and heard behind me a great voice, as of a trumpet, saying, I am Alpha and Omega, the first and the last: and, What thou seest, write in a book, and send it unto the seven churches which are in Asia; unto Ephesus, and unto Smyrna, and unto Pergamos, and unto Thyatira, and unto Sardis, and unto Philadelphia, and unto Laodicea.*

The return of Jesus Christ will be in two stages. The first stage is going to be like a thief in the night. There will be a second stage of the second coming. He will come with those who had already been asleep in the Lord and those who had been raptured. When these two groups are with Him for seven years, a lot of terrible things will be happening on earth. Those on earth during this time will really suffer.

After the seven years, we will now come back with Him to fight the battle of Armageddon. The battle will last for just one day. All the armies of the world will be gathered for this battle. After the battle, we will then reign with Jesus for a thousand years.

The passage above says He is coming with clouds and not in the clouds. What are these clouds? Daniel 7:13-14 provides a clue:

I saw in the night visions, and, behold, one like the Son of man came with the clouds of heaven, and came to the Ancient of days, and they brought him near before him. And there was given him dominion, and glory, and a kingdom, that all people, nations, and languages, should serve him: his dominion is an everlasting dominion, which shall not pass away, and his kingdom that which shall not be destroyed.

Daniel was an exceptionally great prophet. Even before Jesus was born, he had seen His second coming.

Hebrews 12:1 tells us more about these clouds:

Wherefore seeing we also are compassed about with so great a cloud of witnesses, let us lay aside every weight, and the sin which doth so easily beset us, and let us run with patience the race that is set before us.

In Hebrews 11, the Bible lists for us many of the great saints of old: Abraham, Isaac, Enoch and so on. We are told how great they were in faith because they were waiting for something. They were waiting for a promise which they did not get because God wanted to include some other people. He wanted more people to join the clouds, Hebrews 11:39-40 confirms this:

And these all, having obtained a good report through faith, received not the promise: God having provided some better thing for us, that they without us should not be made perfect.

They struggled hard to receive the promise of the Son of man who will come and receive the Kingdom from the Ancient of Days, so that they can reign with Him forever. They had to wait because there were still some people that God wanted to add to the number.

At the second stage of the second coming of Jesus, all of us with glorious bodies, in white linen and on white horses, will follow Him. Anybody looking at us from the ground will see us as clouds moving. Our Captain will be in front. I will be directly behind Him. Where will you be?

The second stage of His second coming will be accompanied by much noise. Every eye will see Him with us. Who are all the eyes that will see us? They will include all the descendants of those who crucified Him. Also, some professing Christians who did not live a holy life and who were therefore left behind will be included. Hebrews 6:4-6 says:

For it is impossible for those who were once enlightened, and have tasted of the heavenly gift, and were made partakers of the Holy Ghost, And have tasted the good word of God, and the powers of the world to come, If they shall fall away, to renew them again unto repentance; seeing they crucify to themselves the Son of God afresh, and put him to an open shame.

Those who are linked with the crucifixion of Jesus are of two categories. The first category includes those who crucified Him more than two thousand years ago. The second category consists of those who are crucifying Him today. This second category, includes some who may call themselves born again but are living an unholy life, and are therefore bad representatives of Jesus Christ; thus they are crucifying Him.

In Revelation 1:8, Jesus introduced Himself as the Alpha and Omega. Alpha is the first letter in the Greek alphabet and Omega is the last letter. When Jesus says He is the Alpha and Omega, it means that He is the beginning and the end. There is no name like the Name of Jesus Christ. He is alive today and He will be alive forever more.

Jesus has never changed. The God of Abraham is still the same God today. The miracles that He performed for Abraham, He can perform for you, today. The God of Daniel, Elijah and Elisha is also my God. What He did for them, He will do for me.

He is not only the One who was and the One who is, but also the One who shall be. This means that the miracles that He performs for us are also available for our children. This is why you should not worry about the future of your children if they belong to God. The best thing that you can give your children is Jesus Christ.

He called Himself the Almighty. At the time that the Book of Revelation was written, the Roman Empire was the largest government in the world. The people who fought against the it were a very small group of Christians with no weapons, no organisation and their leader had already gone to Heaven. How were these people able to overcome the might of the Roman Empire? It was impossible except for one little secret. Their Captain was the Almighty. He is the Alpha and the Omega.

If Almighty God is backing you up, there is no battle that you cannot win. If you have Jesus in your life, you will never be fearful. Unless you are not doing His will, no enemy can overcome you.

THROUGH PATIENCE AND ENDURANCE WE SHALL MAKE HEAVEN

In Revelation 1:9, John introduced himself as *"your brother"*. This means that those who receive His letters are his brothers. Anyone who is going to Hell is not my brother. I am only related to those going to Heaven.

He also said, *" ... your companion in tribulation ... and in the patience of Christ"*. This confirms that he was writing about what he had already experienced. Also, he was aware of passing through tribulations because of Jesus Christ, and with much patience. He is our companion. Someone who does not know sorrow cannot comfort others. 2 Corinthians 1:3 says:

> *Blessed be God, even the Father of our Lord Jesus Christ, the Father of mercies, and the God of all comfort.*

Acts 14:22 says anyone who wants to enter into the Kingdom of God has to pass through tribulations. 2 Timothy 2:12 says that if we suffer we shall also reign with Him and if we deny Him, He also will deny us. If your Christianity is such that the world loves you and you are not persecuted, you have to check yourself. You may not be included among those going to Heaven. If you really stand up for Jesus Christ, persecutions will come. Your friends will desert you, although Jesus Christ never will.

Chapter 4

THE VISION OF THE GLORIFIED CHRIST

Jesus Christ is the Prophet. He is the High Priest. See how He is described in Revelation 1:12-13:

> *And I turned to see the voice that spake with me. And being turned, I saw seven golden candlesticks; And in the midst of the seven candlesticks one like unto the Son of man, clothed with a garment down to the foot, and girt about the paps with a golden girdle.*

John said that he turned to see the voice that was speaking to him. One would have expected him to say that he turned to see the man who was speaking to him. How can anybody see a voice? One can only hear a voice.

However, in certain exceptional circumstances, it is possible to see the invisible. For example, when you are in the spirit, you will see what ordinary eyes cannot see. You will hear what ordinary ears cannot hear. On special occasions, when the Almighty is near, the invisible becomes visible. In Exodus 20:18, it says that the people saw the noise of the trumpet and not that they heard the noise of the trumpet. This was the day that God gave the children of Israel the Ten Commandments. It was a special day.

John went on to say that when he turned to see the voice, he saw certain things. He saw seven golden candlesticks. In the midst of seven candlesticks, he saw someone like the Son of man. This was Jesus. He was clothed in a garment down to the foot and girt about the paps with a golden girdle.

God considered the dress of Jesus so important that He gave a space for it in the Book of Revelation. We will look into the scriptures to see those who have worn this kind of dress before. Our first example is in Daniel 10:5:

Then I lifted up mine eyes, and looked, and behold a certain man clothed in linen, whose loins were girded with fine gold of Uphaz:

Daniel had been fasting for twenty-one days and God sent a messenger to tell him about certain things that would happen. The messenger wore a dress of fine linen, which reached to his feet and a golden girdle about the waist. This dress is a dress of a messenger of God. It is the dress of a prophet.

Another example is in Exodus 28:4:

And these are the garments which they shall make; a breastplate, and an ephod, and a robe, and a broidered coat, a mitre, and a girdle: and they shall make holy garments for Aaron thy brother, and his sons, that he may minister unto me in the priest's office.

Here, we see this same kind of dress worn by a priest. In 1 Samuel 18:4, this kind of dress was also worn:

And Jonathan stripped himself of the robe that was upon him, and gave it to David, and his garments, even to his sword, and to his bow, and to his girdle.

Jonathan was a prince. He wore this same type of dress. We have seen three kinds of people who wore this kind of dress: a prophet, a prince and a priest. In other words, this dress tells us three major things about Jesus Christ. Firstly, that Jesus is the true Prophet. A true prophet of God starts his prophecy by saying, *"Thus says the Lord ... "* Jesus is Lord.

Secondly, we know that Jesus Christ is our High Priest. Who is a Priest? A priest is someone who has access to God. A true priest is someone who can go to God at any time, not only on his own behalf, but also on behalf of others. Jesus Christ said He is the Way, the Truth and the Life and that no man gets to the Father except through Him (John 14:6).

Thirdly, Jesus Christ is the Prince of Peace. He is also the King of kings and the Lord of lords. He is the One who reigns forever. In Revelation 19:16, when John looked a little more closely at the dress of Jesus, he saw an inscription: "KING OF KINGS, AND LORD OF LORDS."

We know, therefore, from the vision that John saw, that right now our Lord and Saviour is no longer hanging on the cross. Those who go about with crosses on their necks saying that it shows that they are close to Jesus must realise that He is no longer on the cross. He is alive for ever more.

If you are still wearing a cross around your neck, it means that you are still relating with the Jesus that was crucified with criminals. Some people wear the cross as a protection against demons. You can do better than this. Surrender your life to Jesus and He will come to you.

As the prophet, He will bring messages to you from God. As the Priest, He will help you take your prayers to God. As the King, He will enable you to reign with Him (Rev. 3:21). In other words, if you are born again, you will be able to tell all the enemies around that you have overcome them because greater is He that is in you than he that is in the world (1 John 4:4).

MEN PROSTRATE BEFORE THE GLORY OF GOD

Let us now look at Revelation 1:14-18:

> *His head and his hairs were white like wool, as white as snow; and his eyes were as aflame of fire; and his feet like unto fine brass, as if they burned in a furnace; and his voice as the sound of many waters. And he had in his right hand seven stars: and out of his mouth went a sharp twoedged sword: and his countenance was as the sun shineth in his strength. And when I saw him, I fell at his feet as dead. And he laid his right hand upon me, saying unto me, Fear not; I am the first and the last: I am he that liveth, and was dead; and, behold, I am alive for evermore, Amen; and have the keys of hell and of death.*

This was the description of the Son of man. This was Jesus Christ in His glorified form. Daniel 7:9 tells us more:

> *I beheld till the thrones were cast down, and the Ancient of days did sit, whose garment was white as snow, and the hair of his head like the pure wool: his throne was like the fiery flame, and his wheels as burning fire.*

Daniel was talking about Jesus. Some say that the Ancient of Days is God the Father. In one sense, it is irrelevant as both Jesus and the Father are God. God the Father is also God the Son. Jesus said that He and the Father are one. In John 14:8-9, Phillip asked Jesus to show him and the disciples the Father. Jesus answered by saying that he who has seen Him has seen the Father.

This figure with a white head and white hair must be very old. This means that the God that I am serving has been in existence for many years. This gives me some comfort. He is older than my problems. This also means that He knows the solution to my problems. The white hair and the white head do not refer to age only but also to experience, wisdom and purity. This means that God is the wisest, the most experienced and the most holy. You should strive to resemble the God that you serve. You should strive to become as wise, as pure and as holy as God, whose eyes were as flames of fire. Let us briefly look at Daniel 10:6:

> *His body also was like the beryl, and his face as the appearance of lightning, and his eyes as lamps of fire, and his arms and his feet like in colour to polished brass, and the voice of his words like the voice of a multitude.*

Daniel described the messenger sent to him. This must have been the Ancient of Days Himself. His eyes were like flames of fire. There was a time when the eyes of Jesus were as blue as the sky. His eyes were full of love. There was a time that He wept with these eyes at the tomb of Lazarus.

He is weeping no more . He is now the King of kings and the Lord of lords. When He returns, those eyes will be full of judgement for all those who reject Him. I thank God that I am going to be at the right side of Jesus Christ on that day. When Jesus comes back to judge the world, anyone who looks at His eyes will shake with fear.

His feet were as burnished brass. This is the description of the divine messenger. Whenever God talks about brass, He is referring to strength. The feet of Jesus are described as strong brass. This means that He has sufficient strength to tread on His enemies. His enemies will be His footstool (Hebrews 1:13). Since we all seated with Jesus in the heavenly places, far above principalities and powers, all our enemies are also under our feet. The devil is under my feet. What about you? Thank God, I belong to Jesus.

John said His voice was like the sound of many waters. At the return of Jesus Christ, when He speaks, the whole world will hear Him. His voice will be like the voice of a judge about to deliver a verdict. On that day, those who have been saying that Jesus is not the Son of God and that He is not the Way to Heaven will all stand before Him, waiting to hear His voice. In one word, He will just say "Guilty".

He had seven stars in His hands. The seven stars stand for the seven pastors of the churches to which He wrote. God is the controller of all stars. Because He controls the stars, He can confuse diviners. Those who look at the stars to prophesy have missed the point. Jesus Christ can re-arrange the stars and say that it is going to be well with you.

From His mouth was the twoedged sword with which He will use to smite His enemies.

The Bible says in 2 Thessalonians 2:8,

> *And then shall that Wicked be revealed, whom the Lord shall consume with the spirit of his mouth, and shall destroy with the brightness of his coming:*

When God is about to finish the battle of Armageddon, He will speak and His enemies will be wiped out. There is something beautiful about the word that comes out of His mouth if you are His child. The Bible says that He sent His word and He healed them (Psalm 107:20). The word that He sent to His enemies is the same word that He will send to heal His children.

His face was shinning like the sun in its strength. Judges 5:31 says:

So let all thine enemies perish, O LORD: but let them that love him be as the sun when he goeth forth in his might. And the land had rest forty years.

The enemies of God will perish but His friends will be like the sun shining in its power.

John said that when he turned and saw Jesus, he did not look like the Jesus that he knew. He used to recline at the bosom of Jesus. John was so shocked that he fainted. Whenever the glory of God comes down, human beings will bow before Him. It is a good thing to see the glory of God. You must, however, expect the unexpected. Saul of Tarsus was arrogantly going to Damascus to persecute Christians but he met Jesus on the way and he fell. When you come into contact with the Almighty God, it will be like a storm battering a lone tree.

Do not be afraid of the glory of God. When the glory of God comes, your sickness will be healed. The problem that the devil has put on you will cease, for it is written that at the Name of Jesus, every knee should bow (Philippians 2:10).

Chapter 5

LETTERS TO THE CHURCHES

Revelation 1:17-20: and 2:1-7

> *And when I saw him, I fell at his feet as dead. And he laid his right hand upon me, saying unto me, Fear not; I am the first and the last: I am he that liveth, and was dead; and, behold, I am alive for evermore, Amen; and have the keys of hell and of death. Write the things which thou hast seen, and the things which are, and the things which shall be hereafter; The mystery of the seven stars which thou sawest in my right hand, and the seven golden candlesticks. The seven stars are the angels of the seven churches: and the seven candlesticks which thou sawest are the seven churches.*

When John saw Jesus Christ in His glorified form, he fainted. Jesus touched him and told him not to fear. *"Fear not"* was a common phrase of Jesus. He said it many times. There was a time when He walked on sea, and when His disciples saw Him, they were afraid. This event is recorded in Matthew 14:26-27. If you find yourself in a storm, do not be afraid, be it a financial storm, a physical storm or a spiritual storm. Jesus is telling you to be of good cheer and fear not.

On the Mount of Transfiguration, when He showed His glory to the disciples that were with Him and they fell at His feet, He told them not to be afraid. Why was He always using this phrase? It is simply because He is Love, and *"fear not"* is the language of love.

This is confirmed in 1 John 4:18:

> *There is no fear in love; but perfect love casteth out fear: because fear hath torment. He that feareth is not made perfect in love.*

If you see an angel in a vision, you will be frightened because angels are huge and powerful. If the angel is from God, he will tell you not to be afraid. However, if the angel smiles and allows you to suffer in fear, then you can be sure that he is from the devil, no matter what his message.

In Revelation 1:18, Jesus said He is alive forever more. He was alive, died, rose again and will never die again. Hell and Death have their own gates. Hell has already broken down its own gate. It has even enlarged its entrance. Once upon a time, Death had its own gate and key (Psalm 9:13). When people are sick, they gradually drift towards the gate of death. When they get to the gate and there is nobody to rescue them, the gates will open, they will roll in and then the gates will close behind them. This is why those who die are gone forever. However, if they call the Name of Jesus before the gate of death opens, He will send His word to heal and deliver them.

As a matter of fact, for those of us that are Christians, the Bible says Jesus has abolished death (2 Timothy 1:10). In those days and even up till now, those who are not Christians are filled with great fear at the point of death. They do not want to die because they know what is waiting for them on the other side. For Christians, even before death comes, death has lost its sting.

One thing that I have noticed about men and women who die in the Lord is that some months or weeks before they die, they lose interest in the world. Also, you will see the yearning in them like someone who wants to go on a journey, like the excitement of visiting a place for the first time.

In Revelation 1:19 it is revealed to us that the Book of Revelation is divided into three parts. Firstly, are the things that John saw as recorded in Revelation 1 the vision of Jesus Christ, the golden candlesticks and the stars in His hands. Secondly, are the things that will take place between the time when John was writing and when we shall all leave this world to be with Jesus, after the rapture. These are recorded in Revelation chapters 2 and 3. Thirdly, are the things that will be thereafter. These will happen after we have gone. These are recorded in Revelation 4 to the end.

In Revelation 1:20, Jesus referred to the seven stars and the seven golden candlesticks. These are symbols that have been very difficult to explain. Even today, Bible scholars do not agree on what exactly is meant by angels of the churches. Some say because the word *angel*, also means messenger in Greek, they must mean the seven messengers of the churches. A more common opinion is that the angel of the church is the pastor of the church. What is important, however, are the letters written to the churches.

Candlesticks represent the churches themselves. Jesus had already called us the light of the world (Matthew 5:14). We are to shine in this world (Philippians 2:15). We are to shine just like candlesticks.

KEYS TO THE LETTERS

These letters were written to seven churches chosen by the Almighty God because they represent all the strength and weaknesses of Christians down the ages. He wrote letters to each of them and to the body of Christ in general. The letters were also meant for individuals in the churches. Each time you read any of the letters, regard it as a letter from your Husband to you. Who is your Husband? Jesus, of course.

God normally deals with individuals. At the end of every letter, He said:

He that hath an ear, let him hear what the Spirit saith unto the churches. (Revelation 2:7, 11, 17, 29, 3:6, 13, 22)

In Revelation 3:20, He said:

Behold, I stand at the door, and knock: if any man hear my voice, and open the door, I will come in to him, and will sup with him, and he with me.

The message is for individuals. On the day of judgement, you will stand as an individual. We will go to Heaven individually. We will be tried individually. We will be rewarded individually.

LETTER TO THE CHURCH AT EPHESUS

The first letter was written to the church at Ephesus. Revelation 2:1-7:

Unto the angel of the church of Ephesus write; These things saith he that holdeth the seven stars in his right hand, who walketh in the midst of the seven golden candlesticks; I know thy works, and thy labour, and thy patience, and how thou canst not bear them which are evil: and thou hast tried them which say they are apostles, and are not, And hast found them liars: and hast borne, and hast patience, and for my name's sake hast laboured, and hast not fainted. Nevertheless I have somewhat against thee, because thou hast left thy first love. Remember therefore from whence thou art fallen, and repent, and do the first works; or else I will come unto thee quickly, and will remove thy candlestick out of his place, except thou repent. But this thou hast, that thou hatest the deeds of the Nicolaitanes, which I also hate. He that hath an ear, let him hear what the Spirit saith unto the churches; To him that overcometh will I give to eat of the tree of life, which is in the midst of the paradise of God.

In order really to understand this letter, we have to know a little about the city of Ephesus and the church that was there. The city of Ephesus was very large with an excellent harbour. It was known as the marketplace of Asia. It was the banking centre of the whole world at that time because there was a great safe in the temple of Diana in the city from where nobody dared steal. It was therefore a safe place to keep money.

The city of Ephesus was also an important religious city. The temple of Diana was one of the seven wonders of the ancient world. It had over one hundred and twenty pillars which were each 60ft. high. Thirty-six of these pillars were gold-plated. Diana was the goddess of prostitutes, and inside the temple of Diana, there were some sacred prostitutes ready to minister to anybody in the temple. Also, if someone committed a crime and ran into the temple of Diana, no arrests were made. Immorality was the order of the day. This was probably why the first letter went to the city of Ephesus.

However, the church in Ephesus was a very strong one. Paul spent a long time with this church. Timothy was its first bishop and he was a very strong Christian. Other members of the church included Aquila, Priscilla, Apollos and even John. Besides the Book of Revelation, we also learn about the church in Ephesus in the Epistle of Paul to the Ephesians, which tells us about being the Bride of Jesus Christ.

God wrote to the church at Ephesus and He told them that He held the seven stars in His hands. If we agree that the seven stars represent the pastors in the churches, Jesus was saying that the pastors were in His hands and He would take care of them. As a Pastor, if you do not do God's will, He will know immediately because you are in His hands. Jesus Christ also said that He knew the work of the Ephesians. They were hard working, patient and had done a lot of work for God.

He said that He knew that they hated the Nicolaitans just as He hated them too. The Nicolaitans believed that once you were saved you were saved forever and you can go on committing sins. Nowadays, their successors have changed their methods. They now say that nobody can be totally perfect or holy. Jesus loves sinners but He hates sin. The people He hates most are those who want to drag those back into the world who are already with Him.

If you have decided not to make Heaven, go to hell alone and do not strive to take others with you. When you say that nobody can be perfect, it means that you have decided that you are not going to be perfect. You are therefore an agent of the devil.

When Paul bade farewell to the elders of the Ephesian church he could see what will happen in the future. He said in Acts 20:28-30:

Take heed therefore unto yourselves, and to all the flock, over the which the Holy Ghost hath made you overseers, to feed the church of God, which he hath purchased with his own blood. For I know this, that after my departing shall grievous wolves enter in among you, not sparing the flock. Also of your own selves shall men arise, speaking perverse things, to draw away disciples after them.

Today, there are many false prophets and apostles. God has warned us in advance. In 1 Thessalonians 5:21 we are told to prove all things and hold fast that which is good.

In Revelation 2:4, God highlighted a big lapse in the life of the Ephesians. There are several possible interpretations but one thing that is certain is that the love which they had for Jesus, suddenly turned cold. Nowadays, many Christians do things mechanically and the love that joined them to Jesus is no more. There was a time when Israel and God were very close but all of a sudden, the love went cold. In Jeremiah 2:2-5, God asked them what warranted this treatment. It was this same question that He asked the church at Ephesus. God is asking you the same question.

In Revelation 2:5, Jesus asked the church at Ephesus to remember their first works. Recollection of the past can be the first step on the way back to God.

Think of the joy you had when you first became a Christian and notice the difference now, especially if the love has gone cold.

In Luke 15:17, we have the story of the prodigal son who ran away from home. He suffered a lot but he suddenly began to think back to when he was with his father. You too will remember how it was at the beginning. A lot of things may have happened between then and now. There could well have been disappointments. These would have come from men and not from God. Our God never fails.

You have to remember first, then repent and then go back to the first works. However, you have to agree that you were wrong. You have to accept that the fault was yours. It is by doing this that you can make amends.

In the letter, the church at Ephesus was told to " ... *repent and do* ... ". You must repent and then begin to obey Him again. If you had been praying for an hour before you go to bed, and now you pray for five minutes, you must repent, accept you were at fault and begin to do something about it. In Luke 15:18, the prodigal son recognised his fault and went back to his father. Examine your faults. When you get to Heaven and face the judgement seat of God, you are going to be examined as an individual.

The interpretation of Revelation 2:7 is that there are some people with ears but who do not hear. They are deaf, in a manner of speaking. No matter what you tell them it makes no difference. They can never change.

Jesus also talked about the tree of life. The tree of life was planted in the Garden of Eden for Adam and Eve to eat from, one day in the future. They, however, wanted to eat from it before it was time. They ate from the forbidden fruit, and so God drove them out of the garden in order to prevent them from eating from the tree of life. If Adam and Eve had been left in the garden, they would have wanted to eat from the tree of life. If they had done this, they would have lived forever. However, they would have lived forever in pain, sickness and sorrow.

The fruit that Adam and Eve could not eat will be given to the overcomers. I am looking forward to that day. Jesus did not say that the overcomers would eat from the tree of life out of their own volition but that He will give them to eat. When we get to Heaven, Jesus Christ will feed us.

Who are the overcomers? They are those who have fought and won. They fought against the devil and against temptation and remained on top. I am going to be one of them. What about you?

Chapter 6

THE LETTER TO THE CHURCH IN SMYRNA

The letter to the church in Smyrna is contained in Revelation 2:8-11:

> *And unto the angel of the church in Smyrna write; These things saith the first and the last, which was dead, and is alive; I know thy works, and tribulation, and poverty, (but thou art rich) and I know the blasphemy of them which say they are Jews, and are not, but are the synagogue of Satan. Fear none of those things which thou shall suffer: behold, the devil shall cast some of you into prison, that ye may be tried; and ye shall have tribulation ten days: be thou faithful unto death, and I will give thee a crown of life. He that hath an ear, let him hear what the Spirit saith unto the churches; he that overcometh shall not be hurt of the second death.*

Out of the seven churches addressed by the risen Lord, only two passed his examination. He did not find anything against them. One of them was the church at Smyrna. I wish God will write to me and say He has nothing against me.

The Last Days

What made the church at Smyrna so special that God had nothing against them? Of all the cities of Asia, Smyrna was the loveliest. It was an extremely beautiful city, called the ornament, crown or flower of Asia. Smyrna was also a great trading city. It was founded in the year 1000 B.C. and destroyed in 600 B.C. The city, however, was rebuilt after four hundred years. This new city was extremely beautiful.

Jesus Christ told the church at Smyrna that He was the One who was dead but now alive. To the people of Smyrna, this was full of meaning. Smyrna was dead but now alive. The city had a famous street called, *'Street of Gold'*. It had a stadium, a magnificent public library and a building for the performance of music. There were also many temples for all kinds of idols such as Zeus, Zabel, Apollo, Nemesis and Aphrodite.

There were many Jews in this city and they were influential. They also were very hostile to the church. Polycarp, Bishop of Smyrna, was one of the most well-known martyrs who died for Christ. The story of his martyrdom in AD 155 is very interesting.

He was eighty-six years old when persecutors came for him. They wanted to tie him to a stake and burn him. He would only be set free if he denied Jesus. Polycarp said that the Lord had been faithful to him for eighty-six years so why should he deny Him? The fire that was set on him did not burn him. In anger, a soldier stabbed him. So much blood came out of his body that it put out the fire around him. He was not an ordinary man.

It was not an easy thing to be a Christian in Smyrna, yet, the letter to them was full of praise. The church was in trouble at the time the letter was written. God told them that more problems were coming:- tribulations, poverty and imprisonment. God's said that He was aware of their poverty but He also knew that they were rich. The divine definition of wealth is different from ours. Jesus Christ said to His disciples in Luke 6:20-21:

> *… Blessed be ye poor: for your's is the kingdom of God. Blessed are ye*

> *that hunger now: for ye shall be filled. Blessed are ye that weep now: for ye shall laugh.*

Are you going to choose the kingdom of this world or the Kingdom of Heaven? In this world, in spite of recent advances in medical care few people live beyond the age of one hundred years. In the Kingdom of God, however, you will live for eternity. This does not mean that you should pray for poverty, but you should not set your heart on earthly riches.

One of the richest people who ever lived was Abraham. His son, Isaac, inherited all his wealth and became even richer. Jacob, the son of Isaac, was wealthy too. God said that He is the God of Abraham, Isaac and Jacob (Exodus 3:6). This means that God does not detest rich people.

2 Corinthians 6:10 explains that the kind of people that God says are poor, yet rich are those who are making others rich. They are those using whatever they have to spread the Kingdom of God. They are those who help others. All that they have belong to God.

James 2:5 says:

> *Hearken, my beloved brethren, Hath not God chosen the poor of this world rich in faith, and heirs of the kingdom which he hath promised to them that love him?*

They may be poor materially but they are rich in faith. This is why God is making sure that these people became closer and closer to Him every day. Also, those who are poor financially find it easy to rely on God. Poor people, for instance, always believe in divine healing. They are not rich enough to seek for medical attention.

Poor people usually find it easier to praise God. However, do not pray to be poor. Instead, make up your mind before you become rich that whatever God provides for you will not separate you from Him.

In Revelation 2:10, God said that some of the Christians in the church at

Smyrna would be imprisoned for ten days. Some commentators have interpreted this as meaning they will be put in prison for a short time and that when they die, they will go to Jesus. Jesus was telling them that if they did not deny Him even unto death, He would give them the crown of life.

As for the Jews, He called some of their meeting places synagogues of Satan. The Jews were the worst persecutors of the Christians at that time. They handed them over to the authorities. Several times they led mobs to attack Christians and to destroy their property. This is still happening today, even between nominal churches and Pentecostal churches.

The crown of life is the reward for martyrs. Jesus had already experienced the worst that the world could do. He passed through a painful death. This is confirmed in Hebrews 4:14-16:

Seeing then that we have a great high priest, that is passed into the heavens, Jesus the Son of God, let us hold fast our profession. For we have not an high priest which cannot be touched with the feeling of our infirmities; but was in all points tempted like as we are, yet without sin. Let us therefore come boldly unto the throne of grace, that we may obtain mercy, and find grace to help in time of need.

If you are suffering today and you call on Jesus for help, He will understand what you are going through. He will know how to help you. I am sure that Jesus will never leave me. When you are complaining that life is tough for you, always remember that Jesus has gone through something worse. You are not dead yet, so your case is still not too bad. When there is life, there is hope. Jesus, who suffered all things, is now waiting in Heaven to present our case to the Father.

One of the reasons Jesus came to the world was to be able to live like an ordinary human being and to experience all the sufferings we have to endure. He knew what it was to be hungry. God can never be hungry, but when Jesus was alive He was once so hungry that He cursed a fig tree that had no fruit on it (Matthew 21:18-19). If you are hungry and you call upon

Jesus Christ, He will understand your predicament and call on the Father to provide for you.

He also knows what it means to get tired. He was once so tired that He was even asleep during a storm (Matt.8:24-26). He knows what it is to be thirsty. He was thirsty on the cross (John 19:28). He knows what pain is, having been beaten with rods (John 19:3) and having a clump of thorns rammed down onto His scalp (John 19:2). He understands whatever suffering you are going through. Call on Him and He will ask the Father to help you. He has conquered the worst. He had triumphed over pain and death. He has obtained final victory. We have already won because our Captain has already won (Romans 8:35-37).

God said that the church in Smyrna should be faithful till death. Why? Why should a Captain demand loyalty till death from his followers? Simply because this Captain was loyal to His father till death. While praying in the garden of Gethsemane, He said that He did not want to die, but if His father's will so demanded he was willing to do so. (Matt. 26:36-46). Jesus also said that no disciple could be greater than his master. He wants us to be faithful till death.

He has suffered for us and left an example that we should follow (1 Peter 2:21). He wants us to be like Him in all things. Some people want to do greater things than Jesus but they are not willing to suffer as He did. He began His public ministry by fasting for forty days. To be like Him, you have to start like Him.

Paul said it all in Philippians 3:10,

> *That I may know him, and the power of his resurrection, and the fellowship of his sufferings, being made conformable unto his death.*

When all is going on well for Christians, they hardly pray. Christians should not pray that there should be no problems. Without examination, there can be no promotion. Sufferings have to come, but they lead to

The Last Days

promotions. Once upon a time, there were two Christian brothers. They were arrested and asked to deny Jesus or they would be set ablaze. The two of them then agreed between themselves that when the fire was burning, if the grace of God was sufficient, the sign to make was to raise the thumb. They were set ablaze and as the fire was burning, the elder brother raised his thumb and said, "His grace is sufficient". The younger brother replied by raising his two thumbs and said, "His grace is more than sufficient".

Your prayer should be that whatever is coming, you will not deny Jesus Christ. Pray that He will uphold you to the end. His grace is more than sufficient for you.

Chapter 7

THE LETTER TO THE CHURCH IN PERGAMOS

Revelation 2:12-17:

And to the angel of the church in Pergamos write; These things saith he which hath the sharp sword with two edges; I know thy works and where thou dwellest, even where Satan's seat is: and thou holdest fast my name, and hast not denied my faith, even in those days wherein Antipas was my faithful martyr, who was slain among you, where Satan dwelleth. But I have a few things against thee, because thou hast there them that hold the doctrine of Balaam, who taught Balac to cast a stumblingblock before the children of Israel, to eat things sacrificed unto idols, and to commit fornication. So hast thou also them that hold the doctrine of the Nicolaitanes, which thing I hate. Repent; or else I will come unto thee quickly, and will fight against them with the sword of my mouth. He that hath an ear, let him hear what the Spirit saith unto the churches; To him that overcometh will I give to eat of the hidden manna, and will give him a white stone, and in the stone a new name written, which no man knoweth saving he that receiveth it.

The Last Days

The third letter was written to the church in Pergamos. Pergamos was the greatest city in Asia. It was the capital city, with a famous library containing more than two hundred thousand books. It was a great religious centre with two major shrines. One was dedicated to Zeus, the prinipal pagan deity. The second was built for Aslepius who was called "The Saviour." He was supposed to be the healing god. The symbol of Aslepius was the serpent. This was why God referred to Pergamos as the seat of Satan.

Jesus said that although they were sitting on the seat of Satan, yet they did not deny Him. There are certain things to learn from this. First, children of God are not supposed to run from forces of darkness. The Almighty God does not expect us to run from battles, He expects us to stand. Ephesians 6 lists all the components of the armour of God. God has made a protective covering for all parts of the body except for the back. This is because God does not expect us to turn back and run.

A child of God running from Satan is like a hunter running away from animals. I will never run from the devil. If the early Christians had run from the devil, there would have been no Christianity today.

God said Antipas was His faithful martyr. The Greek word for martyr is martus. It means a witness. There is a play on words here. In those days, to witness to Christ meant being ready to die for Christ. The one who will die for Christ is the one who will witness for Christ, no matter the circumstances. Nowadays, people are afraid of facing ridicule.

The Lord said in Matthew 10:32-33:

> *Whosoever therefore shall confess me before men, him will I confess also before my Father which is in heaven. But whosoever shall deny me before men, him will I also deny before my Father which is in heaven.*

God was saying here that if you deny Him before men, when we get to Heaven, He will also deny you in front of the Father. If, however, you confess Him before men, in Heaven, you will be introduced to the Father. You have to make up your mind what to do. Will you deny Him or confess Him? I am sure that those of us who are really determined to confess Him will be strengthened by God to be victorious.

In Revelation 2:14-15, He said He had a few things against the church in Pergamos. The incident mentioned here is found in Numbers 23. The children of Israel were on their way to the Promised Land; conquering nations as they went along. They got to the land of Moab whose king, Balak, out of fear of the Israelites, sent for Balaam, a prophet, to come and curse them. Balaam went to meet Balak even though God told him not to do so. However, Balaam blessed the Israelites instead. As he opened his mouth to curse them, blessings came out instead. When you are on the side of God, any curse pronounced on you by the forces of evil will change to blessings.

When Balaam was asked why he blessed the Israelites instead of cursing them, he said he received commandment to bless from the Lord and he could not reverse it. He said he could not curse them because there was no sin among them.

Balaam then advised Balak to befriend the Israelites and invite them to a feast. He was also told to find some enticing ladies to serve them. The Israelites attended the feast, dined and committed fornication. God became angry with them. What happened next is recorded in Numbers 25:5 and 9. Balaam taught Balak what to do and it worked, with the result that God destroyed twenty four thousand of His own children.

What Jesus meant in Revelation 2:14-15 was that there were some people in the church of Pergamos who were teaching exactly the same thing that Balaam taught Balak. These types of people taught that once you are saved, you can do anything you like. They called themselves the righteousness of God in Christ and said that they can do whatever they like. They say that they can even commit adultery as long as they come back to ask for forgiveness later. They forget that even though God is Love, He is also the consuming fire. Do not play with sin.

In Revelation 2:15, Jesus mentioned the people who followed the Nicolaitans. They were like those who followed the doctrine of Balaam. They were those who compromise and embraced lower standards. Some churches nowadays give you the impression of a hotel. These days, Christians do many dubious things in the name of liberty. They forget that the Almighty God does not lower His standard in order to be modern. He is the same yesterday, today and forever more.

In Revelation 2:16, God said He was coming to fight against those who followed wrong doctrines. God knows how to separate those doing His will from those who are not. In every church in the world, we find a mixture of good and bad people. There will always be those who will hear the word of God and do it wholeheartedly; there will also always be those who do not. God, however, knows how to separate the sheep from the goats.

God saved the Israelites from Egypt but not all of them reached the Promised Land. Not everyone who professes faith will make it to Heaven. As for me, my number one goal is to make Heaven.

In Revelation 2:17, He said that he that overcomes would get three things. Firstly, anyone who overcomes will be given to eat of the hidden manna. Secondly, anyone who overcomes will be given a white stone and thirdly, anyone who overcomes will be given a new name. To explain what hidden manna means, we have to look at Psalm 78:24-25:

> *And had rained down manna upon them to eat, and had given them of the corn of heaven. Man did eat angels' food: he sent them meat to the full.*

Manna is the food of angels. Overcomers will eat this food. However, there is a special hidden manna that we will eat on our wedding day with Jesus.

White is the colour of Heaven; no wonder Jesus talked about a white stone. The scriptures confirm this:

> *He that overcometh, the same shall be clothed in white raiment; and I*

> will not blot out his name out of the book of life, but I will confess his name before my father, and before his angels.

Revelation 3:5

> After this I beheld, and, lo, a great multitude, which no man could number, of all nations, and kindreds, and people, and tongues, stood before the throne, and before the Lamb, clothed with white robes, and palms in their hands;

Revelation 7:9

> And to her was granted that she should be arrayed in fine linen, clean and white: for the fine linen is the righteousness of saints.

Revelation 19:8

> And the armies which were in heaven followed him upon white horses, clothed in fine linen, white and clean.

Revelation 19:14

On the white stone was a new name. In Heaven, everything is new: a new song, a new heaven, a new earth, new Jerusalem. We are also to be given new names.

Already, we were given new names when we became born again but, no one except the owner of the name will know the name they will receive in Heaven. Whatever it is going to cost me, I am going to receive my white stone and a new name.

Chapter 8

THE LETTER TO THE CHURCH IN THYATIRA

Revelation 2:18-29:

And unto the angel of the church in Thyatira write; These things saith the Son of God, who hath his eyes like unto a flame of fire, and his feet are like fine brass; I know thy works, and charity, and service, and faith, and thy patience, and thy works; and the last to be more than the first. Notwithstanding I have a few things against thee, because thou sufferest that woman Jezebel, which calleth herself a prophetess, to teach and to seduce my servants to commit fornication, and to eat things sacrificed unto idols. And I gave her space to repent of her fornication; and she repented not. Behold, I will cast her into a bed, and them that commit adultery with her into great tribulation, except they repent of their deeds. And I will kill her children with death; and all the churches shall know that I am he which searcheth the reins and hearts: and I will give unto every one of you according to your works. But unto you I say, and unto the rest in Thyatira, as many as have not this doctrine, and which have not known the depths of Satan, as they speak; I will put upon you none other burden. But that which ye have already hold fast till I come. And he that overcometh, and keepeth my works unto the end, to him will I give power over the nations: And he shall rule them with a rod of iron; as the vessels of a potter shall they be broken to shivers: even as I received of my Father. And I will give him the morning star. He that hath an ear, let him hear what the Spirit saith unto the churches.

THE CLAIM OF CHRISTIANITY IS THAT JESUS CHRIST IS THE ONLY SAVIOUR

To the smallest church was the recipient of the longest letter. This shows how serious their problem must have been. Thyatira was a great commercial town which specialised in dyeing wool red or purple. This was where Lydia was born. Thyatira had an armed garrison. It had a fortune-telling shrine and a large number of trade unions. You could not sell your goods in the city unless you belonged to one of these trade unions. Members of the unions always held feasts in the temple of their idols and also engaged in gross immorality.

The Christians in this city therefore had problems, especially the traders among them. They had to join the unions if they were to be allowed to trade. To join the unions meant they must participate in idol worshipping and immorality. This put them in a real quandary.

There was a woman in the church that God referred to as Jezebel because she resembled the original Jezebel. She was very influential, rich and called herself a prophetess. She encouraged the brethren in the church at Thyatira to join the unions and partake in the idolatry and immorality. Since she called herself a prophetess, the people took her advice.

In Revelation 2:18, Jesus described Himself as having eyes as red as a flame. This shows that He was seriously angry, although in Revelation 2:19, He congratulated the church on the good things he could see in them: love, service, faith and patience.

However, in Revelation 2:20-21, He said that He had a few things against them. The name Jezebel connotes the devil himself. The original Jezebel was a very evil woman. She brought idolatry into Israel. She killed a lot of the prophets of God. She arranged the murder of Naboth (1 Kings 21).

The church in Thyatira was a wonderful church as far as its fellowship was concerned. There was so much love and care that everything looked fine. However, underneath, there was danger. This happens in many churches today. Just as we talk of congregations with problems, we also have individuals with problems. In the church, they appear to be saints but deep within them, they are wicked. You cannot deceive Jesus Christ. If you do not want to follow Jesus all the way, do not follow Him at all. Do not pretend.

It is a terrible thing to appear as a child of God when in fact you are a child of the devil. Poison is more dangerous when it is not labelled as poison. Some professing Christians are poison yet they parade themselves as saints. The Bible says that a servant cannot serve two masters (Matthew 6:24). You either serve Jesus or mammon. There are some people who say there are many ways to Heaven. This is not true. Jesus is the only Way. Acts 4:12 says:

> *Neither is there salvation in any other: for there is none other name under heaven given among men, whereby we must be saved.*

People always quarrel with us when we say Jesus is the only Way. They ask that if Jesus is the only way, what is going to happen to the others? However, if the owner of a house says there is only one way to his house, it is stupid to argue with him as to whether it is so. God says Jesus is the way and He shows the way to everybody. God so loved the world that He gave His only begotten Son and that whosoever believes in Him will not perish but have everlasting life (John 3:16). The choice that God gave the Israelites, in the days of old, is the same choice He offers today. He says that you should choose whom you would serve. (Joshua 24:15).

For my family, and me we will serve the Lord.

PUNISHMENT OF A SIN IS ALWAYS IN PROPORTION TO THE SIN

Why was God angry with Jezebel? Jezebel used three weapons against the children of God. One was food. The devil is still using this weapon against the children of God today. Some people are not serving God the way they ought to because they are eating too much. Food and the stomach will perish one day. The most important food is the food of life, which is the word of God for it lasts forever.

Her second weapon was sex. This is a very big problem today, especially with young people. They are filled with immoral thoughts. If you really love Jesus, when immoral thoughts begin to come, it is a warning that your love for Him may be beginning to get cold and therefore you need a new touch from the Holy Spirit.

Thirdly, she used wealth. Everyone desires to be rich. There is nothing wrong with this. Poverty is not good. The devil knows this so he tries to make people rich overnight. Money obtained through the devil, however, will not be spent judiciously.

God told us what was to happen to Jezebel if she did not repent (Revelation 2:22-23). When God wants to punish someone, the punishment is always related to the sin committed. The Bible contains several examples of this. Gehazi's punishment was related to his sin. He collected goods and money from Naaman on behalf of Elisha without Elisha's consent. Elisha had cured Naaman free of charge (2 Kings 5:16). Gehazi wanted profit from his master's kindness. Instead, he became a leper and indeed had to go and live apart from his fellows because lepers in those days did not live in the city. In 1 Kings 22:38, dogs licked the blood of Ahab just as God has prophesied through Elijah, following the murder of Naboth (1 Kings 21:19)

The world is changing everyday and new things are coming in, particularly into the Church. Some people talk of "old-fashioned" Christianity. They forget that God is the same yesterday, today and forever. If this makes Him appear old fashioned, so be it.

In Revelation 2:26-28 we find promises to those who overcome. These promises are overwhelming. First, they will rule nations. When Jesus comes again, we will rule with Him. He will be in Jerusalem, which will be the capital city and we will reign over the entire world.

Secondly, the overcomers will receive the morning star. The morning star used to be the original name of Satan. He used to be called Day Star. If you overcome; Lucifer will, become your dog.

When we get to Heaven, having won many souls on earth, we will shine as stars (Daniel 12:3). However, some stars will shine brighter than others. Stars do not shine during the day. However, in Heaven, some stars will shine so much that they will be visible even in the day time.

The new name of Jesus is *"The bright morning Star"*. This means that if you overcome, He will give you Himself. No other reward can be greater than this.

Chapter 9

THE LETTER TO THE CHURCH IN SARDIS

Revelation 3:1-6:

> *And unto the angel of the church in Sardis write; These things saith he that hath the seven Spirits of God, and the seven stars; I know thy works, that thou hast a name that thou livest, and art dead. Be watchful, and strengthen the things which remain, that are ready to die: for I have not found thy works perfect before God. Remember therefore how thou hast received and heard, and hold fast, and repent. If therefore thou shalt not watch, I will come on thee as a thief, and thou shalt not know what hour I will come upon thee. Thou hast a few names even in Sardis which have not defiled their garments; and they shall walk with me in white: for they are worthy. He that overcometh, the same shall be clothed in white raiment; and I will not blot out his name out of the book of life, but I will confess his name before my Father, and before his angels. He that hath an ear, let him hear what the Spirit saith unto the churches.*

The letter to the church in Sardis was a very sad one indeed. With the exception of a few in Sardis who did not soil their garments, as it were, the Lord had nothing good to say about them. For the other churches, at least, there were a few positive features to commend them for. Not a single commendation was given to the church at Sardis.

In order to understand this letter, we have to know a little bit about the history of Sardis. Seven hundred years before the letter was written, Sardis was one of the greatest cities in the world. It was a wealthy city with a river full of waters of gold. The greatest king of Sardis, Croesus, was the richest man ever to have lived up to that time.

The city was built on a hill so steep that the inhabitants thought nobody could conquer them because of the natural defence. On two occasions, they were attacked and surrounded by enemies. Instead of fighting back, they went to sleep thinking that they were totally safe. They woke up the next morning to see that the city had been captured.

Even after the city was rebuilt after an earthquake destroyed it in AD.17, the people still remained lazy. They were very rich, living in idle leisure. Initially, the church in the city was strong but a time came when they became like the people around them. They became lazy and prayerless.

This is true of many Christians today. Many children of God are lazy. Even our Lord and Saviour, Jesus Christ, learnt how to work with His hands. Paul the Apostle worked with his hands. There are many Christians today who pay people to pray for them. Some even pay people to fast for them. There are certain things which Almighty God expects you to do yourself. These include praying, fasting, working in the house of God with your hands, witnessing and preaching to others.

In Revelation 3:1, Jesus introduced Himself as having seven Spirits of God. Isaiah 11:1-2 states the things that the Holy Spirit will do in our lives:

And there shall come forth a rod out of the stem of Jesse, and a Branch shall grow out of his roots: and the spirit of the LORD shall rest upon him, the spirit of wisdom and understanding, the spirit of counsel and might, the spirit of knowledge and of the fear of the LORD;

There are seven major areas where the Holy Spirit operates in the life of a person. This means that we call the Holy Spirit by seven names. It also means that when you have the Holy Spirit, you have all the seven virtues: spirit of the Lord, wisdom, understanding, counsel, might, knowledge and the fear of the Lord.

These virtues are linked together. For example, the fear of the Lord is the beginning of wisdom. In other words, the spirit of the fear of the Lord is the same as the spirit of wisdom. Also, wisdom is not greater than might. If you are wise, you are a mighty man therefore the spirits of might and wisdom are the same thing.

God has the Holy Spirit in full. The same Holy Spirit that dwells in Jesus Christ can dwell in you also, if you want Him. If you surrender to Him fully, He will dwell in you fully. If you limit Him, He will not force Himself on you.

The Lord said that the brethren at Sardis were alive but dead. A life totally devoted to pleasure is a life of sin. It is a life of death. A lot of Christians live a dead life because they love pleasure.

But she that liveth in pleasure is dead while she liveth. 1 Timothy 5:6

Continual watchfullness is the price for salvation. In Revelation 3:2, He warned the church that they should be watchful. The greatest need for a Christian is watchfulness. You are to watch all the time. It is the time that you think you do not need to pray or fast that you are closest to your destruction.

The Bible says that we should take heed so as not to fall (1 Corinthians 1:12). Many times, Christians have failed to watch. The devil likes to strike when you have just won a victory. After Elijah killed the prophets of Baal, he thought that he could relax. Then the devil attacked him through the threats of Jezebel. Elijah had to run (1 Kings 19:1-14). In fact, he asked God to kill him. Romans 13:11 says:

And that, knowing the time, that now it is high time to awake out of sleep: for now is our salvation nearer than when we believed.

Satan knows when you are about to reach your goal and this is when he will try to set his biggest trap. Let us hold fast to what we have. Christians must watch out on five fronts. First, you must watch against the wiles of the devil.

Be sober, be vigilant; because your adversary the devil, as a roaring lion, walketh about, seeking whom he may devour. 1 Peter 5:8:

Second, watch against temptations. They cannot but come.

Watch and pray, that ye enter not into temptation: the spirit indeed is willing, but the flesh is weak. Matthew 26:41:

Third, you must watch out against false teaching.

For I know this, that after my departing shall grievous wolves enter in among you, not sparing the flock. Also of your own selves shall men arise, speaking perverse things, to draw away disciples after them. Acts 20:29-30

Fourth, you must watch out against sub-standard service to God. Some people serve God from their armchairs. They have forgotten that Jesus Christ worked physically when He was on earth. God is going to judge our service.

Be watchful, and strengthen the things which remain, that are ready to die: for I have not found thy works perfect before God. Revelation 3:2

Fifth, you must watch out for the coming of the Lord. He said He will come like a thief in the night. It is only those who are watching that will be ready when He comes.

Watch therefore: for ye know not what hour your Lord doth come. But know this, that if the good man of the house had known in what watch the thief would come, he would have watched, and would not have suffered his house to be broken up. Matthew 24:42-43:

THERE WILL ALWAYS BE A FEW WHO ARE TOTALLY DEVOTED TO GOD

In Revelation 3:4, the Lord said there were a few names even in Sardis that had not defiled their garments. God was saying that hopeless as Sardis was, there were still some people who did His will. I am sure that these people would have been called fanatics by the others.

God will always find a few, anyway. Are you going to be among the few? This question should provoke trembling into your heart. If you are found among the few, when the judgements of sinners comes, you will not be condemned. It has happened before, according to 1 Kings 14:13:

And all Israel shall mourn for him, and bury him: for he only of Jeroboam shall come to the grave, because in him there is found some good thing toward the LORD God of Israel in the house of Jeroboam.

Jeroboam had many sons. He was evil. God planned to wipe out his whole family violently, but to exempt one son who would die naturally. His name was Abijah. He was the only one in the family doing the will of God. God took him to be with Him before the blood bath that wiped out the rest of the house of Jeroboem.

Those doing the will of God wholeheartedly will not be around during the time of the tribulation. Some people will be left behind to receive the kind of letter that the church in Sardis received. They will call themselves the living church, but God will tell them that they are dead. The Lord said the few shall walk with Him in white because they are worthy. God was saying that during the banquet in the air, we shall be in white robes. In the ancient times, a white robe signified a lot of things. White robe stood for festivities, as we read in Ecclesiastes 9:8:

Let thy garments be always white; and let thy head lack no ointment,

Also, white robes stood for victory. In those days, after a battle had been won, warriors changed into white robes. God was saying that the few who will remain faithful to Him will wear the attire of a victor. Furthermore, white robes stood for purity. When you were pure, you wore white. Those who will wear white are those who are pure in heart because they will see God.

Chapter 10

LETTER TO THE CHURCH IN PHILADELPHIA

Revelation 3:7-13:

And to the angel of the church in Philadelphia write; These things saith he that is holy, he that is true, he that hath the key of David, he that openeth, and no man shutteth; and shutteth, and no man openeth; I know thy works: behold, I have set before thee an open door, and no man can shut it: for thou hast a little strength, and hast kept my word, and hast not denied my name. Behold, I will make them of the synagogue of Satan, which say they are Jews, and are not, but do lie; behold, I will make them to come and worship before thy feet, and to know that I have loved thee. Because thou hast kept the word of my patience, I also will keep thee from the hour of temptation, which shall come upon all the world, to try them that dwell upon the earth. Behold, I come quickly: hold that fast which thou hast, that no man take thy crown. Him that overcometh will make a pillar in the temple of my God, and he shall go no more out: and I will write upon him the name of my God, and the name of the city of my God, which is new Jerusalem, which cometh down out of heaven from my God! and I will write upon him my new name. He that hath an ear, let him hear what the Spirit saith unto the churches.

The letter to the church in Philadelphia reads beautifully. There were no rebukes – only praises in it. The church was given several promises. The only warning given to them was that they should hold fast.

Let us quickly look at the history of Philadelphia and see how it affected the church. Philadelphia is a Greek name and means the city of brotherly love. The city was founded mainly to spead Greek culture and language to the surrounding cities. The only problem the city had was that it was caused by the widespread cultivation of grapes, which made wine cheap and readily available. It was thus not unusual to find people already drunk in the morning.

In AD. 17, the earthquake that shook Sardis also affected Philadelphia. The tremors in Philadelphia continued for several years. The frequent tremors kept them constantly alert. The city had changed its name several times. At a time when Caesar helped them, they changed the name of the city to New Caesarea. Later, during the reign of the emperor Vespasian, it was re-named Flavia, after Flavius (the emperor's family name), in gratitude for the help he gave them. It was then changed back to Philadelphia. Jesus promised new names to those who overcome when they get to Heaven.

The church in Philadelphia was an extremely strong one because it was a missionary-minded church. The members were always witnessing and sending people out on missions. When the Mohammedans came to Asia Minor and all the other churches collapsed, the church in Philadelphia stood firm. They told the Mohammedans that they would not convert to Islam but rather, the Mohammedans should become Christians. Today, there is still a church in Philadelphia. The fact that God had no rebuke for them is a great lesson to us. It means that if you are constantly winning souls for Christ, Satan will not be able to tarnish you.

In Revelation 3:7, Jesus called Himself holy and true. The word *holy* also means different. It means something separate and distinct. Isaiah 40:25 says:

To whom then will ye liken me, or shall I be equal? saith the Holy One.

The holiness of God makes Him different from the false gods of paganism. This means that every child of God must be different from the children of the world. The Bible says that we are a peculiar people (1 Peter 2:9). We must be peculiar in everything. Even birds know their own kind. Children of God should flock together.

If you long to be blessed or you want anything, you can get it through Jesus Christ. This is why I pity Christians who rush out in the morning without praying. The way to all God's goodness is through Jesus. Start your day with Him and you have already had a success that day.

In Revelation 3:8, He said that He had set before them an open door which no man can shut, for even though they had little strength, they had still kept His word. With your little strength, if you have Jesus backing you up, you will be more successful than someone with strength but without the backing of Jesus. Everything will become easy when God is backing you.

He said no one can shut the door that He opens. If God is the One who has opened a door for you, no wicked person can close it no matter how much they try. When God wants to raise you up, nobody can hold you down. This is why you must go about His business without fear.

What are the kinds of doors that God will open for you? One is the door of missionary opportunities.

But I will tarry at Ephesus until Pentecost. For a great door and effectual is opened unto me, and there are many adversaries. 1 Corinthians 16:8-9

Paul said he would spend more time at Ephesus because even though there were many enemies around, God had given him several opportunities to witness there. God has a way of rewarding those who are witnessing for Him. He gives them more opportunities to witness. The most difficult soul to win is the first one. After this, it becomes easier and easier. God will open the door for you to win more souls. John 15:1-2 says:

I am the true vine, and my Father is the husbandman. Every branch in me that beareth not fruit he taketh away: and every branch that beareth fruit, he purgeth it, that it may bring forth more fruit.

There is also the door of prayer. It is open to everybody. Anybody can pray. Nobody can stop you from praying. Even if there is a government decree against prayer, those who are determined to pray will still pray. Any government who promulgates this type of decree must be ready to awake at all hours because some of us will be ready to wake up at 3 a.m. to pray.

In Revelation 3:9, Jesus gave some promises. There were several promises that the Lord made to the children of Israel. After a while, they lost their special relationship with God and He created a new Israel, which He called Israel of God. This consists of the born again Christians, and is mentioned in Galatians 6:15-16:

For in Christ Jesus neither circumcision availeth any thing, nor uncircumcision, but a new creature. And as many as walk according to this rule, peace be on them, and mercy, and upon the Israel of God.

Galatians 3:28-29:

There is neither Jew nor Greek, there is neither bond nor free, there is neither male nor female: for ye are all one in Christ Jesus. And if ye be Christ's, then are ye Abraham's seed, and heirs according to the promise.

All of us who are in Christ shall inherit all the promises of Abraham. Let us look at two of these promises. Firstly, Isaiah 60:14 says:

The sons also of them that afflicted thee shalt come bending unto thee; and all they that despised thee shall bow themselves down at the soles of thy feet; and they shall call thee, The city of the LORD, the Zion of the Holy One of Israel.

All those who had at one time oppressed the children of Israel will one day come and bow at their feet. Secondly, Isaiah 49:23:-

And kings shall be thy nursing fathers, and their queens thy nursing mothers: they shall bow down to thee with their face toward the earth, and lick up the dust of thy feet; and thou shalt know that I am the LORD: for they shall not be ashamed that wait for me.

The Jews were given all these precious promises. The Jews are still expecting the day when all Gentiles will come and bow down to them. They do not know that things have changed. The promises have now been transferred to the Church. Any Jew that does not accept Jesus Christ as their Lord and Saviour is going to bow down to those of us who are Christians. All those persecuting the Church today will one day bow the knee.

One of the promises that God gave to the church in Philadelphia was that He would keep them from the hour of temptation which shall come. This time of trouble is the time of tribulation. There are three schools of thought on this. One says that Christians will go through the tribulation. The second says that Christians will go through only three and a half years of tribulation before God takes them away. The third says that Christians will not be around when the trouble starts.

The greatest support for the third school of thought is found in Revelation 3:10. Jesus said if you keep His word, you will be kept from the trouble that is coming. He gave a warning even to the church at Philadelphia that they must hold fast to what they have so that no one would take their crowns. This message is also for us.

Here is a true story. Once upon a time, in a Communist state, fifty Christians were being tortured. The soldiers torturing them took them to a lake of freezing water and stripped them naked. Near the lake, they made a large bonfire. The idea was that when any of the Christians decided to deny Jesus, they would be allowed out of the lake to go near the bonfire to warm themselves up. These Christians, however, resisted. Suddenly, fifty angels appeared with crowns in their hands and moved towards the Christians.

It was at this very moment that one of the Christians could no longer resist the pains. He could no longer hold fast so he started moving out of the water. The angel who brought his own crown became sad and was about to move back to Heaven when one of the soldiers stripped himself naked and claimed the crown meant for the Christian who surrendered.

So hold fast to what you have or else someone else will claim your crown. Let us ask God to remove any temptation that will make us deny Jesus Christ and lose our crown.

CHAPTER 11

LETTER TO THE CHURCH IN LAODICEA

Revelation 3:14-22:

And unto the angel of the church of the Laodiceans write; These things saith the Amen, the faithful and true witness, the beginning of the creation of God; I know thy works, that thou art neither cold nor hot: I would thou wert cold or hot. So then because thou art lukewarm, and neither cold nor hot, I will spue thee out of my mouth. Because thou sayest, I am rich, and increased with goods, and have need of nothing; and knowest not that thou art wretched, and miserable, and poor, and blind, and naked: I counsel thee to buy of me gold tried in the fire, that thou mayest be rich; and white raiment, that thou mayest be clothed, and that the shame of thy nakedness do not appear; and anoint thine eyes with eyesalve, that thou mayest see. As many as I love, I rebuke and chasten: be zealous therefore, and repent. Behold, I stand at the door, and knock: if any man hear my voice, and open the door, I will come in to him, and will sup with him, and he with me. To him that overcometh will grant to sit with me in my throne, even as I also overcame, and am set down with my Father in his throne. He that hath an ear, let him hear what the Spirit saith unto the churches.

Laodicea was a great banking and financial centre. The city was so rich its inhabitants felt that they did not need God. It was also a great centre of textile manufacture, and a very important medical centre that specialised in eye and ear treatment.

Every member of the church at Laodicea was wealthy. They therefore felt that with money, they could buy anything. They had plenty clothes so there was no question of nakedness. They had specialised medical scientists. They were also very proud people. Out of the seven churches, it was only the church at Laodicea that Jesus had nothing good to say about. Sardis, bad as it was, still had some good people.

What was the problem with the Laodiceans? They were lukewarm. They were indifferent. They were neither hot nor cold. Jesus will not tolerate being lukewarm. Thirty years before this letter was written, Paul the Apostle wrote to the bishop of the church whose name was Archippus. This is in Colossians 4:16-17:

And when this epistle is read among you, cause that it be read also in the church of the Laodiceans; and that ye likewise read the epistle from Laodicea. And say to Archippus, Take heed to the ministry, which thou hast received in the Lord, that thou fulfil it.

Archippus ignored this letter and everything went downhill. Thirty years later, God saw nothing good in the church. Let us look at the titles that Jesus Christ gave Himself in this letter. He called Himself, Amen. Amen means, so let it be. In those days, it was used as a signature. Amen is the signature of God on all His promises. 2 Corinthians 1: 19-20 says:

For the Son of God, Jesus Christ, who was preached among you by us, even by me and Silvanus and Timotheus, was not yea and nay, but in him was yea. For all the promises of God in him are yea, and in him Amen, unto the glory of God by us.

In other words, provided you have Jesus Christ as the signature, all the promises of God will come to pass in your life.

He also called Himself the faithful witness. There are different types of witnesses. Some speculate on what Heaven looks like. However, Jesus Christ is the faithful and true witness. He confirmed this in John 3:12-13:

If I have told you earthly things, and ye believe not, how shall ye believe, if I tell you of heavenly things? And no man hath ascended up to heaven, but he that came down from heaven, even the Son of man which is in heaven.

When Jesus talked about heavenly things, He was not talking of things that He thought might be there, He was talking of things that He knew are there. He revealed to us that there are many mansions in His Father's house (John 14:2). He knew what He was talking about.

In the letter to the Laodiceans, He said He is the beginning of the creation of God. It is written that in the beginning was the Word, the word was with God and the Word was God (John 1:1). It is this Word, that made things. Later on, according to the Bible, the Word became flesh and dwelt among us. This Word is Jesus Christ.

He is the One who made all things. He is the firstborn of every creature. If Jesus is the beginning of all things it means that He can supply body spare parts for our healing. He can overhaul our system.

IT IS IMPOSSIBLE TO BE INDIFFERENT TO CHRIST

God said that the church at Laodicea was neither hot nor cold. He said that He knew their works. God detests neutrality. You are either for Him or you are not. If you do not walk along the one way to Heaven, you have missed the road. If you try to go another way, you are surely on your way to Hell.

If you are in a boarding house in a school, for instance, you have to abide by all the rules governing the house. Christians have decided to be boarders of Jesus Christ. Jesus will not force you to become a Christian but once you decide to be a Christian, you are in the boarding house of God. If you play truant, you will get into serious problems.

Psalm 91:1 says:

He that dwelleth in the secret place of the most High shall abide under the shadow of the Almighty.

God will protect anyone living in His boarding house. If you do not want the shadow of God to cover you, He will not quarrel with you. However, once you choose Christ, you also choose everything that goes with Him.

In Revelation 3:17, in the letter to the Laodiceans, He said they thought that they were rich. As far as God was concerned, however, they were wretched, miserable, poor, blind and naked. This is the description of every Christian that is lukewarm, especially if it is due to being rich.

You may know the story of the fool in Luke 12:16-20. He had such great wealth that he told his soul to relax and be merry. God called him a fool. If God calls a man a fool, he must be a fool indeed. God said he would leave the world that very day and it was so. The moment you think you do not need God, the devil will move in. My prayer is that we never reach that stage where we will say we do not need God.

He went on to say that they were naked even though they had great clothes. There are several meanings to this. In the world today, those who think that they wear the best clothes are the ones who look almost naked. Those of us who have Christ do not need the best clothes to make us look important. When God wants to honour a man, He will clothe him with salvation.

In Revelation 3:18 Jesus said the church in Laodicea should ask Him for gold that is tried in fire. Let us look at 1 Peter 1:7 for the meaning of this:

That the trial of your faith, being much more precious than of gold that perisheth, though it be tried with fire, might be found unto praise and honour and glory at the appearing of Jesus Christ.

The best gold, which has been tried in the fire, is faith in Almighty God. Faith that God will meet all your needs is the gold that will never perish. If you have everything and you do not have faith, you actually have nothing. Without faith, you cannot please God.

Jesus went on to say that the church at Laodicea should buy from Him eye drops to clear their eyes. All the time, they were doing wrong but did not realise it. They did not stop anybody from preaching yet they were lukewarm. They did not know that they were doing anything wrong. Many of us are like this.

John 9:40-41 says:

And some of the Pharisees, which were with him, heard these words, and said unto him, Are we blind also? Jesus said unto them, If ye were blind, ye should have no sin: but now ye say, we see; therefore your sin remaineth.

May Almighty God open our eyes so we may know whether we are lukewarm or not because we have to discover this before we can amend our ways. We have to accept that we are wrong before we can change.

THERE IS NO TRUE LOVE WITHOUT DISCIPLINE

In Revelation 3:19 Jesus went on to say that He rebukes those that He loves. The Greek word for rebuke means to compel a man to see the error in his ways. God wants to make us see our errors ourselves. It is those that He loves that He disciplines.

The Bible says that if someone is doing something wrong and you do not discipline him, it means that you hate them. Look at Proverbs 13:24:

He that spareth his rod hateth his son: but he that loveth him chasteneth him betimes.

The Bible shows us clearly that when God wants to give the final punishment to someone, He will say that they should be left alone. This is what He said about Ephraim in Hosea 4:17:

Ephraim is joined to idols: let him alone.

When God says you should be left alone, it means He has washed His hands of you. May God never wash off His hands of us.

Jesus went on to say that He was standing at the door, knocking. He is still at the door knocking. You may either open the door to Him or shut Him out. He will not compel you. Just remember that a day is coming when you will knock at the door of Heaven and all your education and wealth will not help you.

In Revelation 3:21, there is a wonderful promise to overcomers. They will sit with Jesus on His throne just as He is now sitting with His father. God and the Holy Spirit are on their thrones. Surrounding these thrones are the four living beings and the twenty-four elders while the angels are one thousand miles away.

When we get to Heaven, there will be some people who will sit about a million miles from the throne. Some will be able to come close to the throne. There will be those who will sit near the throne and those who will sit on the throne itself. These are the overcomers.

You are not an overcomer until you have fought. We have a lot of fighting to do. The Bible says that from, the day of John the Baptist until now, the Kingdom of God suffers violence and, the violent have taken it by force (Matthew 11:12). To become an overcomer, you cannot afford to be lukewarm. God has to revive you. You cannot be neutral towards Christ.

Chapter 12

THE DOOR OF REVELATION

In the first three chapters of the Book of Revelation, we are introduced to the glorified Christ and then to the letters to the seven churches. In the fourth chapter, we are introduced to another realm of revelation. Revelation 4:1-11:

> *After this I looked, and, behold, a door was opened in heaven: and the first voice which I heard was as it were of a trumpet talking with me; which said, Come up hither, and I will show thee things which must be hereafter. And immediately I was in the spirit: and, behold, a throne was set in heaven, and one sat on the throne. And He that sat was to look upon like a jasper and a sardine stone: and there was a rainbow round about the throne, in sight like unto an emerald. And round about the throne were four and twenty seats: and upon the seats I saw four and twenty elders sitting, clothed in white raiment; and they had on their heads crowns of gold. And out of the throne proceeded lightnings and thunderings and voices: and there were seven lamps of fire burning before the throne, which are the seven Spirits of God. And before the*

throne there was a sea of glass like unto crystal: and in the midst of the throne, and roundabout the throne, were four beasts full of eyes before and behind. And the first beast was like a lion, and the second beast like a calf, and the third beast had a face as a man, and the fourth beast was like a flying eagle. And the four beasts had each of them six wings about him; and they were full of eyes within: and they rest not day and night, saying, Holy, holy, holy, Lord God Almighty, which was, and is, and is to come. And when those beasts give glory and honour and thanks to him that sat on the throne, who liveth forever and ever, The four and twenty elders fall down before Him that sat on the throne, and worship Him that liveth forever and ever, and cast their crowns before the throne, saying, Thou art worthy, O Lord, to receive glory and honour and power: for thou hast created all things, and for thy pleasure they are and were created.

John looked up after the dictation of the letter to the seven churches and he saw a door open into Heaven. The voice that talked to him told him to come up and see certain things. The early chapters of the Book of Revelation introduce us to three doors. The first one is in Revelation 3:8 where the Lord said that He had set an open door, the door of prayer and missionary activity – for the church at Philadelphia. In Revelation 3:20, we meet the door of choice. The third door is this one in Revelation 4:1.

This is the door of heavenly revelation. When the doors of Heaven open, you will see beautiful things. Many of us are so busy looking at the things of the world that we never have any opportunity of seeing a vision of Heaven. Whenever you look upwards and take your heart away from material things and begin to think of Heaven and the second coming of Jesus, you will begin to see visions of Heaven. If the door of Heaven should open, you are likely to see visions of God. Ezekiel 1:1 says:

Now it came to pass in the thirtieth year, in the fourth month, in the fifth day of the month, as I was among the captives by the river of Chebar, that the heavens were opened, and I saw visions of God.

When Stephen looked up, he saw a vision of God the Son (Acts 7:56). When Jesus was being baptised, He saw Heaven open and saw the vision of the Holy Spirit (Mark 1:10). When you begin to think about heavenly things, you will begin to see heavenly visions.

John was told to come and see things that would happen hereafter. Up to Revelation 3, the Book of Revelation addressed the churches. From Revelation chapter 4 to chapter 14, nothing is heard about the churches. This is another proof that the Church is going to be taken away before the tribulation. From Chapters 4 to 19 are the record of the tribulation that will happen in this world. During this period of seven horrible years, there is not a single mention of the Church on earth.

In Revelation 2-3, the phrase, "He that hath an ear, let him hear what the Spirit saith unto the church" occurs at the end of each letter. In Revelation 13:9 when this phrase comes up again, there is no mention of the Church. This is because at the end of Revelation 3, just as the door opens in Heaven, the Church is taken away.

John said he was in the spirit (Revelation 4:2). Our present bodies cannot go to Heaven as they are unless they are transformed into spirits. Even now, you have to be in the spirit before you can be able to see heavenly things.

In Revelation 2 and 3, we are introduced to a throne and its surroundings. In Revelation 4, the first thing that John saw was a heavenly throne. We all know that God has a Throne. Isaiah 6:1 confirms this:

> *In the year that King Uzziah died I saw also the Lord sitting upon a throne, high and lifted up, and his train filled the temple.*

John did not bother to describe to us something that he did not see too clearly. Instead, he described the glory of God. It looked like a jasper, pure, bright, and glorious and without any blemish at all. This stands for the overwhelming radiance of the holiness of God.

John described the glory of God as sardine or sardius stone. This has a very deep colour. This could be referring to the blood of Jesus. He also saw a rainbow round the throne with the colour of emerald. Emeralds are green in colour. Green stands for power, productivity and mercy. All this refers to the Holy Spirit.

Revelation 4:4 introduces us to certain things around the Throne of God. John saw twenty-four elders on twenty-four seats. God always surrounds Himself with a group of people called elders. They can be called the Supreme Council of God.

Some scholars say that these elders are the twelve patriarchs and the twelve apostles. If this is so, then how come that John, who was one of the twelve apostles and still on earth, could have seen twelve apostles round the Throne of God? The best conclusion is that twelve of the elders represent the Jews and the other twelve represent Christians. When we get to Heaven we shall know the reality of this image.

In Revelation 4:5, John said that out of the throne proceeded lightnings, thunderings and voices. Anytime that God comes down, for example, in the Old Testament, there will be lightning, thunder and voices. These are always connected with the presence of God.

Heaven is a noisy place. This is why any church, where He is truly worshipped, should not be dull. If everything is cold, you can be sure that God is not there! Those who are really full of life cannot keep quiet for long.

In Revelation 4:6, John saw a sea of glass like crystal. The word 'sea' in the Bible, is always used to represent human beings. A restless sea is a very good picture of human beings. The particular sea before the Throne of God was at rest. It was like a sea of glass and as clear as crystal. Bible Scholars believe that this is a picture of the saints, all dressed in white, at rest before God. This particular sea had no storms. When we get to Heaven, there will be no more problems and we will be at rest.

John went on to describe four beasts full of eyes. One was like a lion, another like an ox, the third like the face of a man and the fourth like a flying eagle. Who were these four beasts? They were Cherubs. The Bible makes it clear that God dwells among the cherubs. Psalm 80:1 for instance says:

> *Give ear, O Shepherd of Israel, thou that leadest Joseph like a flock; thou that dwellest between the cherubims, shine forth.*

The cherubim are the bodyguards of God. They are mighty and extremely strong angels. The Bible says that when God wants to go somewhere, He rides on a cherub. This is in Psalm 18:10,16.

> *And he rode upon a cherub, and did fly: yea, he did fly upon the wings of the wind.*

TRUE CHRISTIANITY IS TOTAL SUBMISSION

Let us now take note of the order of things in Heaven. First is the Throne of God with God on it. Next to Him are the four living beings. These are the mighty cherubs. Next are the twenty-four thrones and the twenty-four elders. We shall come across the other things later.

Some Bible scholars believe that the three cherubim also represent various aspects of Jesus Christ. The lion is said to represent Jesus as the Lion of Judah. The ox represents Jesus as the ideal and perfect Man. Lastly, the eagle represents Jesus as the One who has origin in Heaven.

These cherubim, we are told, sing an anthem of praise. They praise God for three main reasons. Firstly, because He is holy. Secondly, because He is the Almighty, and thirdly, because He lives for ever. Each time that the living beings praise God, the twenty-four elders join them.

They come down from their thrones, remove their crowns and lay them at the feet of the Almighty. They worship and praise Him because He is the Creator of all things and we are created for His pleasure.

We have a lesson to learn from these twenty-four elders. When they want to praise God, they come down from their thrones. You cannot really praise God if you do not first submit yourself. You have to come down from your throne. You have to lay all your achievements at the feet of the One who made them possible.

Let us join the twenty-four elders in worshipping, and glorifying God; singing to Him from the bottom of our hearts. Let us forget who we are, lift Him high and magnify His holy name. He is worthy to be magnified.

Chapter 13

JESUS CHRIST IS THE LAMB AND THE LION

Revelation 5:1-14:

And I saw in the right hand of him that sat on the throne a book written within and on the backside, sealed with seven seals. And I saw a strong angel proclaiming with a loud voice, Who is worthy to open the book, and to loose the seals thereof? And no man in heaven, nor in earth, neither under the earth, was able to open the book, neither to look thereon. And I wept much, because no man was found worthy to open and to read the book, neither to look thereon, And one of the elders saith unto me, Weep not: behold, the Lion of the tribe of Judah, the Root of David, hath prevailed to open the book, and to loose the seven seals thereof. And I beheld, and, lo, in the midst of the throne and of the four beasts, and in the midst of the elders, stood a Lamb as it had been slain, having seven horns and seven eyes, which are the seven Spirits of God sent forth into all the earth. And he came and took the book out of the right hand of him that sat upon the throne. And when he had taken the book, the four beasts and four and twenty elders fell down before the Lamb, having every one of them harps, and golden vials full of odours, which are the prayers of saints. And they sung a new song, saying, Thou art worthy to take the book, and to open the seals thereof: for thou wast slain, and hast redeemed us to God by thy blood out of every kindred, and tongue, and people, and nation; And hast made us unto our God kings and priests: and we shall reign on the earth. And I beheld, and I heard the voice of many angels round about the throne and the beasts and the elders: and the number of them was ten thousand times ten thousand, and thousands of thousands; Saying with a loud voice, Worthy is the Lamb that was slain to receive power, and riches, and wisdom, and strength, and honour, and glory, and blessing. And every creature which is in heaven, and on the earth, and under the earth, and such as are in the sea, and all that are in them, heard I saying, Blessing, and honour, and glory, and power, be unto him that sitteth upon the throne, and unto the Lamb for ever and ever. And the four beasts said, Amen. And the four and twenty elders fell down and worshipped him that liveth forever and ever.

In Revelation 5:1, what John saw was not a book as we know it but a scroll of paper. In the those days, they wrote scrolls and not books. The longer the content, the longer was the scroll. For example, the Gospel of St. Mark was a scroll 19 feet long. While, the Gospel according to St Matthew was 30 feet long; The Book of Revelation was 17 feet long.

This particular scroll that John saw was in God's hand. He saw the book in the hand of the One who sat on the throne – in other words God. At least we have now discovered that God has a hand. There were seven seals on this particular scroll. In times past, when someone wanted to write a will, they had to have seven witnesses present. When the will was to be read out, the seven witnesses had to be present.

Here was a book with seven seals in the hand of God. This was the will of God for the end of the age. God told Daniel about this even before the birth of Jesus Christ, in Daniel 12:8-10:

And I heard, but I understood not: then said I, O my Lord, What shall be the end of these things? And he said, Go thy way, Daniel: for the words are closed up and sealed till the time of the end. Many shall be purified, and made white, and tried; but the wicked shall do wickedly: and none of the wicked shall understand; but the wise shall understand.

In Revelation 5:2, a strong angel came forth. Every angel is supernaturally strong. An ordinary angel could kill at least 185,000 soldiers in one night (2 Kings 19). You can only imagine what a strong angel must be like. He had to be strong enough to make an announcement that would be heard throughout the universe. When He lifted up his voice and shouted, everybody heard him. He called on anyone worthy to open the book and the seals.

In Revelation 5:3-5, we read about the dilemma in which John found himself. He was excited when he first saw the scroll with seven seals but he became depressed and even wept when nobody came to open the book. In Revelation 4:1, the one who called John to look up to Heaven had already informed him that he would see a lot of things. However, it seemed that all his hopes were frustrated.

In Amos 3:7, God promised that He will never do anything without revealing it to His servants the prophets. Here, nobody was worthy enough to receive information from God. The world had become so terrible that God could not find a single man to whom He could talk. Our present world is moving steadily towards this type of situation. God can trust very few people now. Even some of those who hear from God twist the message to suit themselves.

While John was weeping, something happened. One of the elders told him to stop weeping. There is a message for many of us in this. We should stop weeping because there is a solution to every problem. Many of us have been weeping because of problems that we cannot understand.

Why was John told not to weep? It was because the Lion of Judah, the

Root of David, prevailed. We also should not weep because Jesus had prevailed. If you had been weeping before you came to Jesus, as soon as you surrendered your life to Him, your weeping should have come to an end because He has prevailed.

He said that in the world there will be tribulations but we must be of good cheer (John 16:33), for He has overcome the world. Jesus has won and we also shall win.

Jesus can open the scroll because of His victory over death. He has overcome all the power of the devil. He has been completely obedient to His Father. Because He has the key of Hell and death, certain things are granted to Him. He has been granted the ability to know God's secrets. He has been granted the privilege to reveal these secrets to people. Let us look at John 12:49-50:

> *For I have not spoken of myself; but the Father, which sent me, he gave me a commandment, what I should say, and what I should speak. And I know that his commandment is life everlasting: whatsoever I speak therefore, even as the Father said unto me, so I speak.*

Jesus Christ has also been granted the privilege to control all things that shall be. He said that all power on earth and in Heaven have been given to Him. He is in control of everything. He is in control of my life so I know that my tomorrow shall be all right.

As John cleared his eyes, he began to see clearly. There are a lot of lessons to learn from this. Whenever you weep, you do not see clearly. If you continue to weep, you will not see what God wants to do next. All the time that John was weeping, he did not know that somebody had come forward to open the book. However, as soon as he dried his eyes, he saw a new scene.

Revelation 5:6 introduces us to a lamb. John saw a lamb with seven horns and seven eyes. The Bible tells us that Jesus is the Lamb of God that came to take away the sins of the world (John 1:29). Isaiah 53:7 also says:

> *He was oppressed, and he was afflicted, yet he opened not his mouth: he is brought as a lamb to the slaughter, and as a sheep before her shearers is dumb, so he openeth not his mouth.*

Jesus is the Lion of Judah, He is the Root of David. He is also the Lamb of God.

Why seven horns and seven eyes? a Horn in the Bible, symbolises power (Deuteronomy 33:17). Seven horns represent perfect power, for Seven is the number of perfection. The Horn also symbolises honour, for example in Psalm 112:9 where David talked about a generous man, he said God would exalt his horn with honour.

The eye symbolises an ability to see. Seven eyes represent perfect vision. This means that the Lamb with seven eyes can see everything, anywhere, Zechariah 4:10 says:

> *For who hath despised the day of small things? for they shall rejoice, and shall see the plummet in the hand of Zerubbabel with those seven; they are the eyes of the LORD, which run to and fro through the whole earth.*

The picture of the Lamb is that of a being who is all-powerful, all glorious and all seeing.

THE PRAYERS OF SAINTS BECOME FRAGRANCE IN HEAVEN

Revelation 5:7 and 8 introduce us to another dimension. The Lamb came forward confidently, to take the book from the hand of God. As this happened, the four living beings and the twenty-four elders knew that the one in control of everything had come. They came forth with their harps ready to praise Him.

The elders also had vials in their hands. Inside each vial was a kind of aroma, which was the prayer of saints. This means that each time you pray after becoming a Christian, your prayers ascend to Heaven. The elders collect them and store them so that God will smell a beautiful fragrance.

Revelation 5:9-10 says that the elders began to sing new songs. We are going to sing new songs when we get to Heaven. The Bible is full of passages urging us to sing new songs for example Psalm 33:3:

Sing unto him a new song; play skilfully with a loud noise.

Psalm 40:3:

And he hath put a new song in my mouth, even praise unto our God: many shall see it, and fear, and shall trust In the LORD.

and Psalm 98:1:

O sing unto the LORD a new song; for he hath done marvellous things: his right hand, and his holy arm, hath gotten him the victory.

The elders and the living creatures sang an anthem to the Almighty. They praised the Lamb because He died. Also, because He died, certain things happened. Firstly, we were restored to God. Secondly, we were delivered from slavery to Satan, and thirdly we are, now made kings and priests of God and we shall reign on earth.

Revelation 5:11-12 mentions the voices of many angels. The angels were so numerous that John could not even hazard a guess of their number. They were countless. They were worshipping God with a loud voice. They were saying He is worthy to receive power. Power belongs to God. 1 Corinthians 1:24 tells us that Jesus Christ is the power of God.

Jesus is also worthy to receive riches. The Bible tells us in Ephesians 3:8 that the riches of Jesus are unsearchable. He is also worthy to receive wisdom. The Bible tells us that Jesus is the wisdom of God (1 Corinthians 1:24). He is also worthy to receive strength. The Bible tells us that Jesus is the strong

One (Psalm 24:8). Jesus Christ is also worthy to receive honour. The Bible says that at the name of Jesus, every knee should bow (Philippians 2:10).

In Revelation 5:13-14, suddenly, an anthem began that was sung by all, including those in Hell. You may wonder why those in Hell should also sing. The Bible says that every tongue shall confess that Jesus Christ is the Lord (Romans 14:11).

If you do not praise Him when you are at peace, you will praise Him when you are in trouble. If you do not call Him Lord now, you will call Him Lord when you get to Hell. Even Satan will bow to Him.

Chapter 14

ISRAEL'S MISSING WEEK

The Book of Revelation is divided into sections. Chapter 1 describes to us the glory of the risen Christ. Chapters 2 and 3 contain the letters to the churches. Chapters 4 and 5 tell us what will be going on in Heaven after the Church has been raptured. Chapters 6 to 19 tell us what will happen to those who are left behind.

Revelation 20 tells us what will happen to the devil when he is imprisoned, that the Book of Life will be opened and all mankind will be divided into those who are fit to go into the Kingdom and those who will go into the lake of fire. Finally in Revelation 21-22 we read about a new earth and a new Heaven.

Before the nation of Israel was taken into captivity in Babylon, Jeremiah spoke. He gave a prophecy from God. Jeremiah 25:11:

> *And this whole land shall be a desolation, and an astonishment; and these nations shall serve the king of Babylon seventy years.*

At the time when Jeremiah spoke, the kingdom of Judah appeared to be very prosperous. There was no sign of impending trouble. However, God said that the whole nation would go into captivity for seventy years and it happened exactly the way God said it.

Among those who were taken into captivity was Daniel. During the sixty-eight years of captivity, Daniel prayed constantly to know the exact time of freedom. This is like Christians today asking God to tell them categorically when Jesus Christ will come back. Daniel prayed for twenty-one days and the answer came. However, when the answer came, he got more than that which he asked. Daniel 9:20-27:

> And whiles I was speaking, and praying, and confessing my sin and the sin of my people Israel, and presenting my supplication before the LORD my God for the holy mountain of my God; Yea, whiles I was speaking in prayer, even the man Gabriel, whom I had seen in the vision at the beginning, being caused to fly swiftly, touched me about the time of the evening oblation. And he informed me, and talked with me, and said, O Daniel, I am now come forth to give thee skill and understanding. At the beginning of thy supplications the commandment came forth and I am come to shew thee; for thou art greatly beloved: therefore understand the matter, and consider the vision. Seventy weeks are determined upon thy people and upon thy holy city, to finish the transgression, and to make an end of sins, and to make reconciliation for iniquity, and to bring in everlasting righteousness, and to seal up the vision and prophecy, and to anoint the most Holy. Know therefore and understand, that from the going forth of the commandment to restore and to build Jerusalem unto the Messiah the Prince shall be seven weeks, and threescore and two weeks: the street shall be built again, and the wall, even in troublous times. And after threescore and two weeks shall Messiah be cut off, but not for himself: and the people of the prince that shall come shall destroy the city and the sanctuary; and the end thereof shall he with a flood, and unto the end of the war

desolations are determined. And he shall confirm the covenant with many for one week: and in the midst of the week he shall cause the sacrifice and the oblation to cease, and for the overspreading of abominations he shall make it desolate, even until the consummation, and that determined shall be poured upon the desolate.

Daniel wanted to know the time of freedom and God told him that because He loved him, He would show him mighty things. God said that He would do mighty things during seventy weeks in the history of the nation of Israel. In the first seven weeks, Jerusalem would be rebuilt. During the next sixty-two weeks, the Israelites will be living on their own land before the Messiah comes. When He comes, He will be killed. Then there will be one week when another prince will come to destroy various things.

Two years after God spoke to Daniel, the king of the Medes and Persians who was holding the Israelites captive, freed them and told them to go and rebuild their land. It is difficult to believe that a man will just set his slaves free. However, when God has decided to set you free, no man can hold you.

The Jews went back to Jerusalem and began to rebuild their land. It took them forty-nine years to do this. Forty-nine is what God called seven weeks, which is forty-nine days. God called His one year, one day. Thus, it is easy to understand the prophecy given to Daniel. The period between the time that the king of Babylon set the Jews free to the day that Jesus rode into Jerusalem is exactly four hundred and eighty three years. This is sixty-nine weeks of God. God said that as soon as you see the Messiah, He would be cut off. No sooner had they started singing, 'Hosanna in the highest' that they started shouting, 'Crucify Him'.

There remains one week to be fulfilled and this one week means seven days or seven years. This week is still missing. Many Bible Scholars call this one week the tribulation years. This is what is described in Revelation 6-19.

God said in the prophecy to Daniel that certain things will happen when the nation of Israel begins to dwell in their land again. The one week was missing because forty years after Jesus Christ died, the Jews were scattered all over the world. Now, they have come back to their nation. Therefore, any time from now onwards, the remaining one week may come.

When that one week comes, I am pleased I will be gone because it will be a terrible time. It is called the period of Jacob's trouble. During this one week, God will do certain things. Firstly, God will finish the transgression of Israel. He is going to make an end to all the sins of Israel.

We know that sin can only end in the world when Satan is out of the way. This is not going to happen until Revelation 20 is fulfilled. Revelation 20:1-3 says:

> *And I saw an angel come down from heaven, having the key of the bottomless pit and a great chain in his hand. And he laid hold on the dragon, that old serpent, which is the Devil, and Satan, and bound him a thousand years, And cast him into the bottomless pit, and shut him up, and set a seal upon him, that he should deceive the nations no more, till the thousand years should be fulfilled: and after that he must be loosed a little season.*

Secondly, God says that He is going to bring reconciliation to Israel. Thirdly, the nation of Israel will be born again in one day. Isaiah 66:8:

> *Who hath heard such a thing? Who hath seen such things? Shall the earth be made to bring forth in one day? Or shall a nation be born at once? for as soon as Zion travailed, she brought forth children.*

If God can do this for Israel then He can do it for any nation. The fourth thing that God will do within this one week is that He will bring in everlasting righteousness. When Satan is bound and Israel is born again, Jesus will return again with all of us who would have already gone to be with Him, to reign on earth for a thousand years. During this time, Satan will be in prison. There will be no need for visions during these thousand years because the Lord Himself will be visible to us.

The fifth thing that God will do during this time is that He will anoint the Most Holy as King over the earth. The Bible tells us that the most beautiful temple that the world has ever seen will be built at this time. However, before this wonderful time comes, Israel will have suffered a lot. Those who will be left on earth will suffer terribly.

Revelation 6:1-2 gives details of what will happen after the rapture:

And I saw when the Lamb opened one of the seals, and I heard, as it were the noise of thunder, one of the four beasts saying, Come and see. And I saw, and behold a white horse: and he that sat on him had a bow; and a crown was given unto him: and he went forth conquering, and to conquer.

There were seven seals. When the first seal was opened, there was a voice like thunder from one of the beasts. One of them said, "Come and see". John was already there so it was somebody else that the beast was inviting to the scene. In response to the call, a rider on a white horse came forth with a bow in his hands. He had no arrows. He was given a crown because he came with none. He then went about conquering.

Who is this rider on a white horse, with a bow and no arrows? It is the Antichrist. As soon the Church is gone, the Antichrist will come riding on a white horse as a sign of victory. Every nation will begin to bow to him.

There are a few things to note here. First, the bow is a sign of military power. Secondly, he had no arrows with him. This means that he is not going to conquer by shooting arrows but by using diplomacy. When the Antichrist comes on the stage, he will sue for peace. People will support him and make him their leader. A crown will be given to him but his reign will result in many things that people never bargained for.

Nonetheless, the whole world will be ready for him and they will be happy that the born again Christians have gone. They will think that they have got a wonderful government but something else will however happen. Revelation 6:3-4:

And when he had opened the second seal, I heard the second beast say, Come and see. And there went out another horse that was red: and power was given to him that sat thereon to take peace from the earth, and that they should kill one another: and there was given unto him a great sword.

Just as the nations are relaxing in their so-called peace, trouble will come. Suddenly, the people will realise that the Antichrist has deceived them. There will be those who will insist on supporting him, but also those who will be ready to fight him. This will lead to great wars on earth.

Some people say that the Antichrist has already come during World War II as Hitler. Some others believe that the Antichrist has already been born and that he will start his evil campaign when he becomes thirty years old. They believe the devil will pattern his life like that of Jesus Christ.

In Matthew 24:6-7, Jesus enlightens us more about the coming trouble:

And ye shall hear of wars and rumours of wars: see that ye be not troubled: for all these things must come to pass, but the end is not yet. For nation shall rise against nation, and kingdom against kingdom: and there shall be famines, and pestilences, and earthquakes, in divers places.

And in Matthew 24:15-16:

When ye therefore shall see the abomination of desolation, spoken of by Daniel the prophet, stand in the holy place, (whoso readeth, let him understand:) Then let them which be in Judaea flee into the mountains:

There will be all kinds of wars. The real war that will end all wars will not come until the Antichrist has come. He will make peace with Israel and allow them to rebuild their temple, but later, he will want them to worship him. He will sacrifice pigs on the altar of the temple. This is something that no Jew will ever tolerate. When you see these things happening, know that the end has come.

The Antichrist will ride on a white horse. Although the white horse symbolises peace, the Antichrist will provoke war. As the wars are going on, something else will follow, as described in Revelation 6:5-6:

> *And when he had opened the third seal, I heard the third beast say, Come and see. And I beheld, and lo a black horse; and he that sat on him had a pair of balances in his hand. And I heard a voice in the midst of the four beasts say, A measure of wheat for a penny, and three measures of barley for a penny; and see thou hurt not the oil and the wine.*

When the wars begin, many men will be drafted in the army. There will be nobody to pay attention to agriculture. People will begin to weigh bread before giving anybody to eat. There will only be enough food for single people. There will not be sufficient for families. Oil and wine, however, will not be affected. Luxury goods like whisky, brandy and champagne will be available. Things, that common people need will not be available. Can a hungry man drink whisky?

Something more terrible will then follow. This is recorded in Revelation 6:7-8:

> *And when he had opened the fourth seal, I heard the voice of the fourth beast say, Come and see. And looked, and behold a pale horse: and his name that sat on him was Death, and Hell followed with him. And power was given unto them over the fourth part of the earth, to kill with sword, and with hunger, and with death, and with the beasts of the earth.*

Famine and death will begin to reap their grim harvest. Many people will die in battles and there will be nobody to bury them. This will lead to pestilence. Those who are not killed by the sword will die of pestilence. The irony of it is that this people will suffer before they die and then they will go to Hell. The Bible says here that within a short period of the coming of the Antichrist, a fourth of the whole world will die.

As we will discover later, those who are alive at this time will envy those who are dead. The living ones will want to die but they will not be able to die. They will have to continue with their sufferings. I thank God that I will be gone before then. What about you?

Terrible as this picture looks, it is just the beginning of sorrows. Out of the seventy weeks revealed to Daniel, sixty-nine weeks have already been fulfilled. Definitely, the remaining one-week will be fulfilled. It is going to happen just as the Bible describes it.

If you are already born again, you should be forever grateful to God that you are going to be spared these troubles. If you are not yet born again, or you have a relative who is yet to be born again, you need to do something about it now. Many of us wait for someone else to come and witness to our parents and relatives. If you are raptured and your parents are left behind, they will never forgive you.

As a Christian, you should thank God that you are going to Heaven. Tell the Almighty God that whatever it is going to cost, you long for all the members of your family to be saved. Pray that God uses you to achieve this purpose.

Chapter 15

THE TRIBULATION SAINTS THE REIGN OF TERROR

Revelation 6:9-11

> *And when he had opened the fifth seal, I saw under the altar the souls of them that were slain for the word of God, and for the testimony which they held: And they cried with a loud voice, saying, How long, O Lord, holy and true, dost thou not judge and avenge our blood on them that dwell on the earth? And white robes were given unto every one of them; and it was said unto them, that they should rest yet for a little season, until their fellow servants also and their brethren, that should be killed as they were, should be fulfilled.*

As the fifth seal was broken, the Lord began to reveal to John some other things that would follow. These include the intense Persecution of Christians during the period of the tribulation. After the rapture, those who become Christians will be easily identified.

One of the reasons for this is that they will refuse to worship the Antichrist and they will also refuse to take his mark. Everyone on earth will be asked to take the mark of the Antichrist, which is 666, but the believers will refuse to take it. The persecutors of the Christians at this time will think they are working for God and that those who do not serve Him ought to be killed. Jesus Christ confirmed this in John 16:2:

They shall put you out of the synagogues: yea, the time cometh, that whosoever killeth you will think that he doeth God service.

You will have to make up your mind, if you are left behind, either to take up the mark of the Antichrist and be condemned forever or refuse to follow him and be ready for the tortures that will follow. The only escape from this dilemma is to decide to follow Christ now, one hundred percent.

Many of the Christians that will be around during the time of the tribulation will be killed. In Revelation 6:10, John saw their souls under the altar. They were crying with a loud voice and asking how long their suffering will last. Many of us ask this type of question even now. We ask how long will Christians suffer at the hands of unbelievers. It will not be long. The end of suffering will come soon.

The Christians asked when their blood would be avenged on those on earth. Because they were suffering, they wanted to be avenged. At that time, those who are saved will be saved as if passing through fire. They will be children of fire and everything about them will be fiery. Therefore, they will be right to ask for vengeance on those who causes them such trouble.

God gave them an answer in Revelation 6:10. He gave each of them a white robe and said they should rest awhile for their fellow-martyrs to die before He took action. Many times, when we think that God is slow to solve our problems, we may be misjudging Him. God has His own timetable for everything. Also, if a certain number of people must be killed before the end comes, it follows then that there is also a certain number of people who must be saved before the end comes. Therefore, let us hurry up and proclaim Jesus to these people so that they can come with us.

REIGN OF TERROR

Revelation 6:12-14:

> *And I beheld when he had opened the sixth seal, and, lo, there was a great earthquake; and the sun became black as sackcloth of hair, and the moon became as blood; And the stars of heaven fell unto the earth, even as a fig tree casteth her untimely figs, when she is shaken of a mighty wind. And the heaven departed as a scroll when it is rolled together; and every mountain and island were moved out of their places.*

There have been many earthquakes since the beginning of the world. In the last twenty-five years alone, there have been more earthquakes than at any time since the beginning of the world. This means that things that have never happened before have started to happen. The big earthquake is coming and there is no way that we can stop it. The earth will explode like an over-heated engine. Many years ago, prophets of God prophesied that these things will happen. Joel 2:10 and 31 say:

> *The earth shall quake before them; the heavens shall tremble: the sun and the moon shall be dark, and the stars shall withdraw their shining: The sun shall be turned into darkness, and the moon into blood, before the great and the terrible day of the LORD come.*

Joel was the one who prophesied about the promise of the Holy Spirit (Joel 2). When Joel gave this prophecy, people thought that he was mad. In the period before Christ, only a few people were baptised by the Holy Spirit. However, now, many people are being baptised in the Holy Spirit. Joel's prophecy has come to pass. Joel's second prophecy will therefore also come to pass, without any doubt. The earthquake come and there will be nothing that we can do about it.

In Revelation 6:13 John saw the stars of Heaven fall. The stars are far from earth and they are positioned very precisely, according, to scientists.

However, when the stars begin to fall, it means that law and order has broken down on earth and in Heaven. In Isaiah 34:4 we are told more of what will happen:

> *And all the host of heaven shall be dissolved, and the heavens shall be rolled together as a scroll: and all their host shall fall down, as the leaf faileth off from the vine, and as a falling fig from the fig tree.*

What God told John had been previously revealed to Isaiah a long time ago. The stars will drop. Some scientist have said this is most unlikely because the stars are so far from Heaven that whatever is happening on earth cannot affect them. If this is so, then what did John see? Some Bible scholars believe that what John saw was an array of big bombs dropping from the atmosphere on the earth. This is also possible. The West already has the technology to do this and is planning so-called 'star wars' devices. Once God has spoken, He has spoken.

The Bible says even the heavens would be rolled up as you roll up a mat or a piece of cloth (Revelation 6:14). When a nuclear bomb explodes, it pushes the air on its way aside and it begins to roll like waves on the sea. We are already developing the process to make sure that what God said will happen will surely happen.

God had told Jeremiah long ago some things that will happen at the end of the world. Jeremiah 4:24 says:

> *I beheld the mountains, and, lo, they trembled, and all the hills moved lightly.*

When a bomb is dropped, it will first hit the ground silently before exploding and scattering everything around it. Revelation 6:15-17:

> *And the kings of the earth, and the great men, and the rich men, and the chief captains, and the mighty men, and every bondman, and every free man, hid themselves in the dens and in the rocks of the mountains; And said to the mountains and rocks, Fall on us, and hide us from the*

face of him that sitteth on the throne, and From the wrath of the lamb: For the great day of his wrath is come; and who shall be able to stand?

The end time is going to be one of universal terror. Those left behind will shake in terror. The Bible lists seven categories of these people. They are the kings, great men and women, rich men, the chief captains (military officers that are supposed to be fearless), mighty men, those in bondage (slaves, servants, apprentices for example) and the free. No one is exempted. Everyone will shake with terror. Zephaniah 1:14 says:

The great day of the LORD is near, it is near, and hasteth greatly, even the voice of the day of the LORD: the mighty man shall cry there bitterly.

When the mighty men begin to weep bitterly, something is seriously wrong. The people who will be on earth at this time will be searching for places to hide. They will be looking for holes and caves. Right from the beginning, sin has always caused man to hide away from God (Genesis 3:8). When Adam and Eve sinned, instead of running to God, they hid from Him. Sin is always driving away people from God. Right now, Jesus is still calling us to come to Him. A time is coming when He will not call again.

During the great tribulation, the people left behind will ask the mountains to fall on them and hide them from the Lamb. They will finally realise that the One who is angry is Jesus Christ, the Lamb of God that was slain. Great as their terror would be, however, they will not ask for forgiveness. Instead, they will want to go into hiding.

This attitude is true of many of us. When we sin, instead of going to God to ask for forgiveness, we begin to look for other methods of solving our problems. The gates of mercy are not yet closed. God is still ready to forgive, restore and be merciful. We should pray not to be a part of this tribulation.

Chapter 16

GOD IS THE CONTROLLER OF THE WEATHER

Revelation 7:1-3:

> *And after these things I saw four angels standing on the four corners of the earth, holding the four winds of the earth, that the wind should not blow on the earth, nor on the sea, nor on any tree. And I saw another angel ascending from the east, having the seal of the living God: and he cried with a loud voice to the four angels, to whom it was given to hurt the earth and the sea, Saying, Hurt not the earth, neither the sea, nor the trees, till we have sealed the servants of our God in their foreheads.*

Before the opening of the seventh seal, God allowed another respite. At the end of Revelation 6, by the time that the sixth seal was broken, the Bible tells us that all categories of people had become terrified because of the things that were happening. However, instead of repenting they went to hide from the wrath of God on the hills and mountains.

While this was going on, the angel with the seventh trumpet was getting ready to blow his trumpet to bring more calamities upon the earth. But

God allowed a little respite before the final series of judgement that were to follow. In the passage above we are told that John saw four angels standing at the four corners of the earth, stopping the four winds of the earth from blowing on the earth, the sea or any tree.

You can imagine what would happen if the winds refuse to blow. We can all do without food for a day. There is evidence that people can fast for as long as two hundred and seventy days without food.

There are a very few men on earth who can do without water for more than forty days. However, I do not or know any human being who can do without air for more than forty minutes. You can then imagine the situation if the winds refuse to blow. This could bring a total end to the world within an hour.

It is a common belief among Bible scholars that all the forces of nature are under the control of angels. We have Bible passages to support this claim. These angels that control the wind, fire and the waters are called the angels of service.

Let us introduce ourselves to some of them. Revelation 14:18:

> *And another angel came out from the altar, which had power over fire; and cried with a loud cry to him that had the sharp sickle, saying, Thrust in thy sharp sickle, and gather the clusters of the vine of the earth; for her grapes are fully ripe.*

This is the angel of fire.

Revelation 16:5:

> *And I heard the angel of the waters say, Thou art righteous, O Lord, which art, and wast, and shalt be, because that hast judged thus.*

This is the angel in charge of the waters. We have already been introduced to the angel in charge of the wind in Revelation 7:1-3. It would be wrong, however, to deduce that angels are so important that we should pray to them. The angels of service belong to the lowest cadre of angels. They are the messengers in Heaven. They are so low that they have to be on duty every time. They cannot even keep the Sabbath. I pity you if you ask such angels to come and help you. These angels, according to the scriptures, particularly those in charge of the winds, sweep the way ahead of God when He wants to go on a journey. There are several Bible passages to support this. Nahum 1:3 says:

> The LORD is slow to anger, and great in power, and will not at all acquit the wicked: the LORD hath his way in the whirlwind and in the storm, and the clouds are the dust of his feet.

Jeremiah 4:13:

> Behold, he shall come up as clouds, and his chariots shall be as a whirlwind: his horses are swifter than eagles. Woe unto us! For we are spoiled.

Zechariah 9:14:

> And the LORD shall be seen over them, and his arrow shall go forth as the lightning; and the Lord GOD shall blow the trumpet, and shall go with whirlwinds of the south.

Isaiah 66:15:

> For, behold, the LORD will come with fire, and with his chariots like a whirlwind, to render his anger with fury, and his rebuke with flames of fire.

1 Kings 19:11:

> And he said, Go forth, and stand upon the mount before the LORD. And, behold, the LORD passed by, and a great and strong wind rent the mountains, and brake in pieces the rocks before the LORD; but the LORD was not in the wind: and after the wind an earthquake; but the LORD was not in the earthquake:

The wind cleared the way ahead of the Almighty God but the Lord Himself was not in the wind. The angels of the wind clear the way ahead of God like despatch riders. There are only four of these angels in charge of the winds. This confirms the fact that there are four major winds; from the south, north, east and west. This is further confirmed in Jeremiah 49:36:

And upon Elam will bring the four winds from the four quarters of heaven, and will scatter them toward all those winds; and there shall be no nation whither the outcasts of Elam shall not come.

Meteorologists try to predict the weather but God is the overall controller of the weather because He controls the angels of the winds. It is not the fault of meteorologists if they make mistakes. They predict what science has taught them while God demonstrates that He is the Omnipotent One.

The conclusion to be deduced from this is that if there is any storm in your life, you should call on the controller of storms. I believe that now you understand what happened on that day when Jesus was sleeping in a boat and there was a storm (Mark 4:38-39). His disciples woke Him up and He said, "Peace, be still." The angels of the winds simply recognised the Master's voice.

When the children of Israel reached the Red Sea and they did not know how to cross over, the Lord told Moses to lift up his rod. You should know now that the rod was Jesus. As soon as the sea saw the rod, it opened up for the Israelites to pass through.

As long as you have Jesus and you constantly lift Him up, there will always be a way for you. No matter what anyone says, it is God's word that is final. If you are in the same aeroplane with Jesus you will land safely. If you are in the same boat with Jesus, whatever storm may arise, He will simply say, "Peace, be still" and there will be peace.

Chapter 17

SEALING OF THE TRIBULATION SAINTS

Revelation 7:4-8:

> *And I heard the number of them which were sealed: and there were sealed an hundred and forty and four thousand. Of all the tribes of the children of Israel. Of the tribe of Juda were sealed twelve thousand of the tribe of Reuben were sealed twelve thousand. Of the tribe of Gad were sealed twelve thousand. Of the tribe of Aser were sealed twelve thousand. Of the tribe of Nephthalim were sealed twelve thousand. Of the tribe of Manasses were sealed twelve thousand. Of the tribe of Simeon were sealed twelve thousand. Of the tribe of Levi were sealed twelve thousand. Of the tribe of Issachar were sealed twelve thousand. Of the tribe of Zabulon were sealed twelve thousand. Of the tribe of Joseph were sealed twelve thousand. Of the tribe of Benjamin were sealed twelve thousand*

The first thing we have to note about this sealing is that whenever God wants to judge the earth, He will always preserve some people. Right from

The Last Days

the time of Noah, when God wanted to wipe out the earth with flood, He made sure that at least eight people were safe in the ark.

During the tribulation, there will also be some people that God will preserve. They will be preserved to become the tribulation evangelists. They are going to witness for God during the period of the tribulation and God will protect them until they finish their assignments.

During the time of Elijah, in 1 Kings 19:18, when he thought that he was the only prophet left, the Almighty God told him that He had preserved seven thousand other faithful men and women. In the same manner, during the tribulation, God has decided ahead of time that He will preserve one hundred and forty four thousand Jews. We know that they will be Jews and they will be taken from the twelve tribes of Israel.

The angel with the seal in his hands was from the east. This information is very important because as we know, the sun rises from the east. Also, When Jesus was born, the first people who came to worship Him were wise men from the east (Matthew 2:1-2). Bible scholars believe that there may be a link between this angel with the seal of the Almighty God in His hand and Jesus. We are not sure that it is Jesus who will come to do the sealing but we believe that the angel may come directly from the throne of Jesus.

Note that I have not implied that the throne of Jesus is in the east. However, we have several Bible passages referring to Jesus and the east. One example is in Malachi 4:2:

> *But unto you that fear my name shall the Sun of righteousness arise with healing in his wings and ye shall go forth, and grow up as calves of the stall.*

We all know that Jesus is the Sun of righteousness and that the sun rises in the east. I believe that what the Lord is trying to tell us is that, even at the moment of His tremendous anger, He will be busy working. I also believe that the Son has a peculiar interest in the human race. This is understandable because He made us. He was the One who advised the Trinity that man should be made in their image. He is the Word that made all things (John 1:3).

Even during the period of tribulation, Jesus will be actively interested in those who are left behind. If He is going to be interested in them at that time, how much more is He interested in His People now? You are making a mistake if you think that Jesus has forgotten you. He will never leave you, nor forsake you (Hebrews 13:5).

The seventh angel had the seal of the Living God in his hands. We should note the phrase, "Living God". Isaiah 44:9-18 gives us a terrible picture of gods that are dead. It talks about gods that have mouths but cannot speak, have ears and cannot hear and have eyes that cannot see.

In Joshua 3:10 we read something important about the Living God and His importance to us:

> *And Joshua said, Hereby ye shall know that the living God is among you, and that he will without fail drive out from before you the Canaanites, and the Hittites, and the Hivites, and the Perizzites, and the Girgashites, and the Amorites, and the Jebusites.*

The names here do not matter. What matters is that if the Living God is on your side, your enemies will fail. When some Christians talk about the enemy, you see fear all over them. If we are not careful, some of us will develop hypertension over the thought of the enemy. Let us be careful so that we do not fall into the trap of the enemy.

The enemy knows fully well that we are already conquerors. The enemy knows that this is written in the Bible. He also knows that he cannot defeat us provided we put our trust entirely in the Living God. So, his strategy is to frighten us and at times he causes us to fall.

The Living God gives victory to His children. The story of Sennacherib in 2 Kings 18:17-19:37 illustrates that when God is on your side, you have already won. Most of the time, when God is going to fight for you, you will not have to do any fighting yourself. The Bible tells us in Psalm 42:1-2 that true satisfaction is only to be found by fellowshipping with the Living God. Once you fellowship with Him, you are sure of true satisfaction.

Hosea 1:10 says that when God has made a promise, He will fulfil it. This was the promise He made to Hosea:

Yet the number of the children of Israel shall be as the sand of the sea, which cannot be measured nor numbered; and it shall come to pass, that in the place where it was said unto them, Ye are not my people, there it shall be said unto them, Ye are the sons of the living God.

This promise has been fulfilled. We are the children of the Living God. Those who are going to be safely brought through the tribulation will have seals on their foreheads. In times past, kings wore rings called signet rings. These rings had seals on them. The seals were like a signature and the symbol of the king's authority. There are several examples in the Bible to show the importance of a king's seal. One is in Genesis 41:41-44:

And Pharaoh said unto Joseph, See, I have set thee over all the land of Egypt. And Pharaoh took off his ring from his hand, and put it upon Joseph's hand, and arrayed him in vestures of fine linen, and put a gold chain about his neck; And he made him to ride in the second chariot which he had; and they cried before him, Bow the knee: and he made him ruler over all the land of Egypt. And Pharaoh said unto Joseph, I am Pharaoh, and without thee shall no man lift up his hand or foot in all the land of Egypt.

Bible scholars believe that the only person that the Almighty God can hand over His signet to is Jesus. Today, the seal of God upon every Christian is Jesus. When you surrender your life to Him. the seal of the Almighty God is placed on you. There are three major seals that are available to Christians through Jesus Christ. The first one is the blood of Jesus. In 1 Peter 1:18-19, the Bible says:

> *For as much as ye know that ye were not redeemed with corruptible things, as silver and gold, from your vain conversation received by tradition from your fathers; but with the precious blood of Christ, as of a lamb without blemish and without spot:*

When dealing with people suspected to be demonic, you have to plead the blood of Jesus. You have to say that the blood covers you. By saying this you are affirming that you belong to Jesus and therefore demons should stay away from you. When you are covered in the blood of the Lamb, you are totally committed to Jesus.

The same blood can protect you and your property. You can cover all your properties with the blood of Jesus. When you do this, you are putting the seal of Jesus on them. A couple once came to me who were concerned about constant strange occurrences in their house. I told them always to plead the blood of Jesus on their money and this solved the problem.

If you are not born again, there is no seal on you yet and the blood of Jesus is not available for you. Come to Jesus and let Him wash you in His blood so that when the enemies see you, they will know that you belong to Jesus.

The second seal for Christians is water baptism. Colossians 2:10 and 12:

> *And ye are complete in him, which is the head of all principality and power: Buried with him in baptism, wherein also ye are risen with him through the faith of the operation of God, who hath raised him from the dead.*

Romans 6:3-5:

> *Know ye not, that so many of us as were baptized into Jesus Christ were baptized into his death? Therefore we are buried with him by baptism into death: that like as Christ was raised up from the dead by the glory of the Father, even so we also should walk in newness of life. For if we have been planted together in the likeness of his death, we shall be also in the likeness of his resurrection:*

The third seal available to Christians is the baptism in the Holy Spirit. Ephesians 1:13:

In whom ye also trusted, after that ye heard the word of truth, the gospel of your salvation: in whom also after that ye believed, ye were sealed with that Holy Spirit of promise.

2 Corinthians 1:22:

Who hath also sealed us, and given the earnest of the Spirit in our hearts.

2 Corinthians 5:5:

Now he that hath wrought us for the self same thing is God, who also hath given unto us the earnest of the Spirit.

Ephesians 4:30:

And grieve not the Holy Spirit of God, whereby ye are sealed unto the day of redemption.

The baptism in the Holy Spirit is essential for every Christian. If you have not been baptised in the Holy Spirit, please do not waste time. Get baptised. It is God's own way of saying you are permanently sealed to Him and He will rescue you from all sorts of dangers that you may not even be aware of.

Concerning the number that was sealed, there are certain points to note. The fact that one hundred and forty four thousand Jews were sealed does not make them more special than the Church. We may begin to wonder why only the Jews were sealed. We have to remember that the Church would have already gone at this time. Those ready to go to be with Christ would have gone before the opening of the seventh seal.

There are those who are born into the nation of Israel who, as far as God is concerned, are not even Jews. If you are a Jew physically and not born again, you are not qualified to be called a Jew in the real sense of the word. In Romans 9:6-7, the Bible says:

> *Not as though the word of God hath taken none effect. For they are not all Israel, which are of Israel: Neither, because they are the seed of Abraham are they all children: but, In Isaac shall thy seed be called.*

Also, Galatians 3:29:

> *And if ye be Christ's, then are ye Abraham's seed, and heirs according to the promise.*

He who belongs to Christ is the real Jew. There are Jews who are Jews by birth and there are Jews who are so because they belong to Christ. There are people who are Jews but they are not recognised by God as Jews.

As far as God is concerned, according to Galatians 6:16, the Church is the real Israel of God. The important question is: will any Christian be around at this terrible time of the opening of the seventh seal? You will not be around if you do what God expects of you. You should not be around when the winds refuse to blow. You should have gone to be with the Almighty God.

From the list of the tribes, there are certain points to note. Judah replaced Reuben as number one. This is because of a prophecy that their father gave in Genesis 49:8. When Jacob was about to die, he gathered his children together and prayed for them:

> *Judah, thou art he whom thy brethren shall praise: thy hand shall be in the neck of thine enemies; thy father's children shall bow down before thee.*

Jacob made Judah number one. The Bible did say that the first shall be the last and the last shall be the first (Luke 13:30). It is my prayer that those of us who are called will not end up as the last.

Why did Reuben lose the first position? This is stated in Genesis 49:3-4:

Reuben, thou art my firstborn, my might, and the beginning of my strength, the excellency of dignity, and the excellency of power: Unstable as water, thou shalt not excel; because thou wentest up to thy father's bed; then defiledst thou it: he went up to my couch.

Reuben went to bed with his father's wife. Going through the list of the tribes, you will observe that Dan is omitted and his place taken by Manasseh, the son of Joseph. The reason for this is found in Genesis 49:17:

Dan shall be a serpent by the way, an adder in the path, that biteth the horse heels, so that his rider shall fall backward.

It is believed by many Bible scholars that the Antichrist is not going to be an Arab but a Jew, and that he is going to come from the tribe of Dan. Jeremiah 8:16 confirms this:

The snorting of his horses was heard from Dan: the whole land trembled at the sound of the neighing of his strong ones; for they are come, and have devoured the land, and all that is in it; the city, and those that dwell therein.

Dan is compared to the serpent and we know that serpent is another name for the devil. We also know that the Antichrist is going to be the son of the devil.

Actually, Ephraim should have been in Manasseh's position. In Genesis 48:17-20 we have an interesting story:

And when Joseph saw that his father laid his right hand upon the head of Ephraim, it displeased him: and he held up his father's hand, to remove it from Ephraim's head unto Manasseh's head. And Joseph said unto his father, Not so, my father: for this is the firstborn; put thy right hand upon his head. And his father refused, and said, I know it, my son, I know it: he also shall become a people, and he also shall be great: but truly his younger brother shall be greater than he, and his seed shall become a multitude of nations. And he blessed them that day, saying,

> *In thee shall Israel bless, saying, God make thee as Ephraim and as Manasseh: and he set Ephraim before Manasseh.*

Joseph brought his two sons, Manasseh and Ephraim, to Jacob for blessings. When Jacob wanted to bless them, he crossed his hands so that his left hand was put on the head of the firstborn, Manasseh, while the right hand was put on Ephraim. This was contrary to tradition. The right hand should have been on the head of the firstborn. Ephraim became so great that he thought he no more needed God. God then decided to boycott him.

There are certain lessons to learn from here. Firstly, it is within the power of God to make number one become number two, simply through the blessing of a father. If you please your father, even if you are the youngest child, you can be promoted to the position of the firstborn. Secondly, after God has placed you where you are, through your own actions, you can change yourself to number one or number ten as you wish.

What was the sin of Ephraim? Hosea 4:17:

Ephraim is joined to idols: let him alone.

You cannot reach such a level of backsliding that Almighty God decides He will not bother again about you and regard you as irredeemable. I have had the unpleasant task of burying a man of God about whom God spoke to me a year before he died. God told me that he wanted to be ordained as a pastor at all cost, even though he was not qualified. God said I should ordain him even though he was no longer praying about getting to Heaven. God said I should ordain him so that he could not use my refusal as an excuse on the last day when he fails to make Heaven. I ordained him and he died less than six months later. The point here is that people can backslide to a point where God will let go of them. I pray that this will never be your case.

If you have been placed in the last position by your activities, you can be brought to number one. If you please God, He can lift you up. He can lift the needy person from the dunghill and set him on a throne (Psalm 113:7). Even if it is decreed that you are going to die in poverty, you can change the decree today.

I believe that God is always willing to co-operate with those who are determined at all cost to make Heaven. I also believe firmly that the word of God is true that says from the days of John the Baptist until now, the Kingdom of Heaven suffers violence and the violent take it by force.

Chapter 18

SALVATION IS FROM GOD ALONE

Revelation 7:9-10:

> *After this I beheld, and, lo, a great multitude, which no man could number, of all nations, and kindreds, and people, and tongues, stood before the throne, and before the Lamb, clothed with white robes, and palms in their hands; And cried with a loud voice, saying, Salvation to our God which sitteth upon the throne, and unto the Lamb.*

One hundred and forty four thousand Jews will go throughout the world to evangelise and witness for Christ. What the result of their work will be is stated above. A lot of people will be converted and they will join those of us who have gone to glory already before the trouble started. John saw multitudes that nobody could count, from all nations, peoples and tongues. They were in white robes, holding palm fronds and singing to God. This is the fulfilment of the promise to Abraham in Genesis 12:3:

> *And I will bless them that bless thee, and curse him that curseth thee; and in thee shall all families of the earth be blessed.*

The Last Days

In Genesis 49:10, God made a promise to Judah:

The sceptre shall not depart from Judah, nor a lawgiver from between his feet, until Shiloh come; and unto him shall the gathering of the people be.

We will all be gathered to Jesus Christ. We have something to learn from the song we will be singing in Heaven. Salvation is from God alone. Look at Jeremiah 3:23:

Truly in vain is salvation hoped for from the hills, and from the multitude of mountains: truly in the LORD our God is the salvation of Israel

Also Hosea 13:4:

Yet I am the LORD thy God from the land of Egypt, and thou shalt know no god but me: for there is no saviour beside me.

Revelation 7:11-12:

And all the angels stood round about the throne, and about the elders and the four beasts, and fell before the throne on their faces, and worshipped God, saying, Amen: Blessing, and glory, and wisdom, and thanksgiving, and honour, and power, and might, be unto our God for ever and ever. Amen.

Human beings do not know how to praise God. The difference between how angels praise God and how human beings praise Him is very great. In the passage above, we read that the angels fell on their faces while praising God. They said that blessings belong to God. It is only God that can bless. When God is with you, anything that you touch will be blessed. An example of this is found in Genesis 39:1-5:

And Joseph was brought down to Egypt; and Potiphar, an officer of Pharaoh, captain of the guard, an Egyptian, bought him of the hands of the Ishmeelites, which had brought him down thither. And the LORD was with Joseph, and he was a prosperous Man; and he was in the

> house of his master the Egyptian. And his master saw that the LORD was with him, and that the LORD made all that he did to prosper in his hand. And Joseph found grace in his sight, and he served him: and he made him overseer over his house, and all that he had he put into his hand. And, it came to pass from the time that he had made him overseer in his house, and over all that he had, that the LORD blessed the Egyptian's house for Joseph's sake; and the blessing of the LORD was upon all that he had in the house, and in the field

Everything that Joseph touched became a success.

In Ezekiel 44:30, God gave some special powers to His priests. They can place a blessing on, or lift a blessing off, a person:

> And the first of all the firstfruits of all things, and every oblation of all, of every sort of your oblations, shall be the priest's: ye shall also give unto the priest the first of your dough, that he may cause the blessing to rest in thine house.

When you please a man of God, you should say, 'Amen' if he blesses you in the Name of the Lord. No matter how tough the opposition, you will ride high. God says you must nonetheless play your part if the blessing is to remain with you. Hebrews 6:7-8 and 10 say:

> For the earth which drinketh in the rain that cometh oft upon it, and bringethforth herbs meet for them by whom it is dressed, receiveth blessing from God: But that which beareth thorns and briers is rejected, and is nigh unto cursing; whose end is to be burned. For God is not unrighteous to forget your work and labour of love, which ye have shewed toward his name, in that ye have ministered to the saints, and do minister.

GLORY, WISDOM, THANKSGIVING, HONOUR, POWER AND MIGHT BELONG TO GOD

The angels talked about glory. It is very difficult to describe what exactly we mean by glory. Psalm 19:1 tells us about the glory of God:

The heavens declare the glory of God; and the firmament showeth his handiwork.

If you want to see the glory of God, all you need to do is to look upwards. The heavens are the showroom of His glory. One of the names by which Jesus is known is 'King of Glory'. One of the last prayers of Jesus was that God should give Him back the glory He left behind while coming to earth. This is in John 17:1 and 5:

These words spake Jesus, and lifted up his eyes to heaven, and said, Father, the hour is come; glorify thy Son, that thy Son also may glorify thee: And now, O Father, glorify thou me with thine own self with the glory which I had with thee before, the world was.

All through His life on earth, He made only two requests of His Father. The second one was that if it was God's will, the cup of suffering should be taken away from Him (Matthew 26:42).

In Isaiah 40:6-8, the Bible compares human glory to the glory of God:

The voice said, Cry. And he said, What shall I cry? All flesh is grass, and all the goodliness thereof is as the flower of the field: The grass withereth, the flower fadeth: because the spirit of the LORD bloweth upon it: surely the people is grass. The grass withereth, the flower fadeth: but the word of our God shall stand forever.

The angels also said that wisdom belongs to God. Unless you are a true child of God, you may not know what is meant by the wisdom of God. Many things about God appear foolish, to unregenerate men. However, 1 Corinthians 1:25 says:

Because the foolishness of God is wiser than men; and the weakness of God is stronger than men.

When we talk about salvation in Jesus, it does not make sense to the unregenerate. When we say that there is only one way to Heaven, that does not make sense. That Jesus, with all His power allowed Himself to be crucified does not make sense. That He died and rose three days later does not make sense.

However, God is wiser than men. Because Jesus died and shed His blood, our sins are cleansed. Because He rose from the dead, we are justified. The Holy Spirit came because He rose again.

Without Jesus, you will not be wise. When Christ comes into your life, you will know what is called wisdom. All that you thought that human wisdom could do, but failed to, Jesus will accomplish. God has wisdom. 1 Corinthians 1 :24 says:

But unto them which are called, both Jews and Greeks, Christ the power of God, and the wisdom of God.

Hand over your problems to Jesus Christ. The angels also said thanksgiving belongs to God. Some of us do not know how important thanksgiving is to God. The one who should know is Jesus. Any time Jesus prayed in the public when He was here on earth, He always started by thanking His Father. Look at Matthew 11:25:

At that time Jesus answered and said, I thank thee, O Father, Lord of heaven and earth, because thou hast hid these things from the wise and prudent, and hast revealed them unto babes.

Also John 11:41-42:

Then they took away the stone from the place where the dead was laid. And Jesus lifted up his eyes, and said, Father, I thank thee that thou hast heard me. And I knew that thou hearest me always: but because of the people which stand by I said it, that they may believe that thou hast sent me.

Some do not know for what to thank God. 1 Thessalonians 5:18

In every thing give thanks: for this is the will of God in Christ Jesus concerning you.

Thank God in all situations. Psalm 50:23:

Whoso offereth praise glorifieth me: and to him that ordereth his conversation aright I will shew the salvation of God.

When you thank Jesus, you glorify God. God wants to be glorified. However, there is one situation where thanksgiving is not acceptable to God. This is when it is borne out of pride. Many of us give this type of thanks while giving our testimonies. Any thanksgiving that draws attention to you and not God is unacceptable.

The angels also said that honour belongs to God. He is the only One that can really honour us. When God wants to honour someone, He does it perfectly, promotion comes from God. When you ask God for wisdom to serve Him, He will add honour and riches, just as He did for Solomon (1 Kings 3:11-13).

Jesus said we should seek first the Kingdom of God and His righteousness. After this, wealth, prosperity, honour, fame and other things will be added. You do not have to struggle for them.

The honour of men always creates problems. If it is men who are honouring you, your story will be like that of Naaman in 2 Kings 5:1:

Naaman, captain of the host of the king of Syria, was a great man with his master, and honourable, because by him the LORD had given deliverance unto Syria: he was also a mighty man in valour, but he was a leper.

Every great man in this world who does not know Jesus has flaws.

The angels also said power belongs to God. In Matthew 28:18 Jesus said:

And Jesus came and spake unto them, saying, All power is given unto me in heaven and in earth.

If all power belongs to Jesus, then there is nothing left for the devil. Those of us who belong to God cannot fail because all power belongs to God. When Christians talk, it appears like boasting to non-Christians, but our boasting is about the power which belongs to our Father. What our Father has belongs to us, Matthew 28:19-20 says:

Go ye therefore, and teach all nations, baptizing them in the name of the Father, and of the Son, and of the Holy Ghost: Teaching them to observe all things whatsoever I have commanded you: and, lo, I am with you alway even unto the end of the world. Amen.

God is with us all the time so we cannot fail. The only way to receive power today is through the Holy Spirit (Acts 1:8). Once you have been baptised in the Holy Spirit, whether you know it or not, the power of God is already resting in you. All that is needed of you is to continue to use that power.

The angels also said that might belongs to God. Might is the ability to do whatever you want. God spoke to Abraham in Genesis 17:1:

And when Abram was ninety years old and nine, the LORD appeared to Abram, and said unto him, I am the Almighty God; walk before me, and be thou perfect.

All Christians must go about with their heads up. They must be proud of who they are because our God is the Almighty.

THE WHITE ROBES AND THE BLOOD OF JESUS

Revelation 7:13-14:

> *And one of the elders answered, saying unto me, What are these which are arrayed in white robes? and whence came they? And I said unto him, Sir, thou knowest. And he said to me, These are they which came out of great tribulation, and have washed their robes, and made them white in the blood of the Lamb.*

Those who get to Heaven will be robed in white. In the Bible, robes are always symbolic of human beings. If you do well, your robes are referred to as white. If you are a sinner, your robes are referred to as dirty. Look at Isaiah 64:6:

> *But we are all as an unclean thing, and all our righteousnesses are as filthy rags; and we all do fade as a leaf; and our iniquities, like the wind, have taken us away.*

Our righteousness is compared with filthy rags.

Revelation 19:7-8

> *Let us be glad and rejoice, and give honour to him: for the marriage of the Lamb is come, and his wife hath made herself ready. And to her was granted that she should be arrayed in fine linen, clean and white for the fine linen is the righteousness of saints.*

John was told that the blood of the Lamb washed the white robes of the tribulation saints. This means that there is a special soap or special water, as it were, that can wash all sins and make them clean. This is the blood of Jesus.

Why is the blood very powerful? The secret is found in Leviticus 17:1:

> *For the life of the flesh is in the blood: and I have given it to you upon the altar to make an atonement for your souls: for it is the blood that maketh an atonement for the soul.*

If someone is bleeding and the blood flow is not stopped, they will die. Life flows out through the blood. When your blood is free from infection you will be fine and healthy. When something is wrong with your blood you become very weak.

The life of Jesus is in His blood. As Jesus is Lord, this means that the life of God is in the blood of Jesus. Nothing can be more powerful than the life of God. What makes God Almighty is the blood of Jesus.

When you wash in the blood, you link yourself with the life of God. Once you are covered with the blood, death will run from you. When the devil sees you covered with the blood, he will run. Many Christians do not know the power in the blood of Jesus. Apart from saving you from sin, the blood also protects you from all kinds of dangers.

The saints washed their own robes, in the blood. God provided the blood. Salvation is free. The blood is waiting. The robes are there. You can wash your robes yourself. Come to Jesus because He is the only way.

Let us now look at Revelation 7:15-17:

> *Therefore are they before the throne of God, and serve him day and night in his temple: and he that sitteth on the throne shall dwell among them. They shall hunger no more, neither thirst any more; neither shall the sun light on them, nor any heat. For the Lamb which is in the midst of the throne shall feed them, and shall lead them unto living fountains of waters: and God shall wipe away all tears from their eyes.*

Those who had been washed by the blood and whose robes had been cleaned stood before the throne of God. Jesus told us that the pure in heart are blessed for they shall see God (Matthew 5:8). Perfect bliss is described in several verses in the Bible. For example, Matthew 5:6 says:

> *Blessed are they which do hunger and thirst after righteousness: for they shall be filled.*

Also John 6:35:

And Jesus said unto them, I am the bread of life: he that cometh to me shall never hunger; and he that believeth on me shall never thirst.

God made us for Himself. After He moulded us from the earth He gave us the breath of life. He gave also us a yearning for Him, which can never be satified until we are linked with God again.

When God says that you should come to Him, part of you will want to answer Him. The devil will also advise you to the contrary. A struggle will go on inside you. However, the day that you accept Jesus, peace will come. That which is in you that yearns for to God will be finally linked to Him. The peace of God will then become yours, no matter the circumstances.

Chapter 19

THE JUDGEMENT OF THE TRUMPETS

We will now shift our focus back to what will be happening to those on earth after the Rapture. We will now begin the study of what is called the judgement of the trumpets. We will also see how painful it is to wish to die and be unable to die.

Revelation 8:1-5:

> *And when he had opened the seventh seal, there was silence in heaven about the space of half an hour. And I saw the seven angels which stood before God; and to them were given seven trumpets. And another angel came and stood at the altar, having a golden censer; and there was given unto him much incense, that he should offer it with the prayers of all saints upon the golden altar which was before the throne. And the smoke of the incense, which came with the prayers of the saints, ascended up before God out of the angel's hand. And the angel took the censer, and filled it with fire of the altar, and cast it into the earth: and there were voices, and thunderings, and lightnings, and an earthquake.*

The Last Days

As soon as the seventh seal was opened, there was silence in Heaven. Even the angels stopped singing. The living beings also kept quiet. For half an hour, everything was silent. Even John knew that something terrible was about to happen.

In verse 5, we are told that, the angel added fire to the censer that contained the prayer of the saints and then poured it back on earth. When he did this, there were voices, thundering, lightning and earthquakes. This tells us that when we pray to God, we should not think that He has not heard us. He has heard and the answer will surely come. As a matter of fact, when the answer comes, it will be more powerful than we expect.

In this particular case, the prayers to which the angel was adding fire were the prayers of the saints who were being persecuted. They cried to God longing to know when He will avenge them. God heard their prayers, added fire to it and sent the prayers back to earth.

You should remember that God warns us not to avenge ourselves but to wait for Him to avenge us. When God decides to avenge you, it will be more terrible than that for which you asked. Look at Romans 12:19-20:

> *Dearly beloved, avenge not yourselves, but rather give place unto wrath: for it is written, Vengeance is mine; I will repay, saith the Lord. Therefore if thine enemy hunger, feed him; if he thirst, give him drink: for in so doing thou shalt heap coals of fire on his head.*

The worst punishment that you can mete out to a man who offends you is to tell him that you leave him to God's judgement. The Bible says that it is a fearful thing to fall into the hands of the living God (Hebrews 10:31). Our God is a consuming fire (Deuteronomy 4:24).

It is better even to ask for forgiveness for your enemies than to leave them in the hands of God.

Also, the greatest compliment that you can ever receive is for someone to say that God will thank you. This is the same as saying that God will bless you. This statement will ascend to Heaven, fire will be added to it and the blessings to follow will be so great that you will not be able to handle them.

Seven angels usually stand in the presence of God. They are Uriel, Raphael, Raguel, Michael, Sariel, Gabriel and Reniel. These are not ordinary angels. In the past, these angels had the power to impose curses on human beings. An example is in Luke 1:18-20:

> *And Zacharias said unto the angel, Whereby shall I know this? for I am an old man, and my wife well stricken in years. And the angel answering said unto him, I am Gabriel, that stand in the presence of God; and am sent to speak unto thee, and to shew thee these glad tidings. And, behold, thou shalt be dumb, and not able to speak, until the day that these things shall be performed, because thou believest not my words, which shall be fulfilled in their season.*

Those of us who are born again are superior to angels. Angels are our messengers. If you know anybody who prays to angels, tell the person to come to Jesus for salvation. Once you are born again, you become superior to the angels and you can go where even they cannot go. Hebrews 10:19 and 22 say:

> *Having therefore, brethren, boldness to enter into the holiest by the blood of Jesus. Let us draw near with a true heart in full assurance of faith, having our hearts sprinkled from an evil conscience, and our bodies washed with pure water.*

We can enter into the holiest. We can go and talk to God in a place which even archangels may not enter.

The seven angels were given seven trumpets. What were they doing with the trumpets? Revelation 8:7-12 reveals this to us:

> *The first angel sounded, and there followed hail and fire mingled with blood, and they were cast upon the earth: and the third part of trees was burnt up, and all green grass was burnt up. And the second angel*

sounded, and as it were a great mountain burning with fire was cast into the sea: and the third part of the sea became blood; And the third part of the creatures which were in the sea, and had life, died; and the third part of the ships were destroyed. And the third angel sounded, and there fell a great star from heaven, burning as it were a lamp, and it fell upon the third part of the rivers, and upon the fountains of waters; And the name of the star is called Wormwood: and the third part of the waters became wormwood; and many men died of the waters, because they were made bitter. And the fourth angel sounded, and the third part of the sun was smitten, and the third part of the moon, and the third part of the stars; so as the third part of them was darkened, and the day shone not for a third part of it, and the night likewise.

In the Bible, when a trumpet is blown, it means that God is about to intervene in the affairs of man.

The trumpet is usually used for one of three main reasons. It is usually blown to prepare people, for example, for battle. It is also used to summon people together. For example, when we will be going to meet Jesus, the trumpet will sound and all born again Christians from all over the world will be summoned. The trumpet is also blown to announce the arrival of royalty. 1 Thessalonians 4:16-17:

For the Lord himself shall descend from heaven with a shout, with the voice of the archangel, and with the trump of God: and the dead in Christ shall rise first: Then we which are alive and remain shall be caught up together with them in the clouds, to meet the Lord in the air: and so shall we ever be with the Lord.

When the first angel sounded his trumpet, hail, fire and storms began to descend upon the earth. Something similar to this happened to the Egyptians when the Israelites were in Egypt. The destruction that is coming will happen on a worldwide scale.

When the second trumpet was blown, John saw something like a great

The Last Days

mountain burning and falling into the sea. Bible scholars believe that what he saw was a great hydrogen bomb dropped by the planes of the superpowers. The bombs that fell on Hiroshima and Nagasaki were atomic bombs which, although devasting, cannot be compared with hydrogen bombs.

The third trumpet sounded and John saw a star fall from Heaven. This could be referring to star wars already being planned by the super powers. The fourth trumpet sounded and another bomb was dropped that made all the waters turn bitter. There are many categories of bombs now. Some explode with a bang while others turn water into poison.

As these trumpets were being blown, things were happening on earth. After the fourth trumpet, God decided to hold on. He wanted to warn the people and give them a chance to repent before the last three trumpets were sounded.

In Revelation 8:13 the warning is spelt out:

> *And I beheld, and heard an angel flying through the midst of heaven, saying with a loud voice, Woe, woe, woe, to the inhabiters of the earth by reason of the other voices of the trumpet of the three angels, which are yet to sound!*

Even after this warning, the people still remained stubborn. There are people suffering today and God keeps sending His people to warn them but they remain stubborn. They say that they do not want to become Christians yet their suffering keeps on multiplying, and there are greater sufferings to come.

Let us make a little comparison here. During this period of great disaster on earth, the people in Heaven will be singing and rejoicing. On earth, there will be weeping and gnashing of teeth. Nothing can be more terrible. To escape this terrible state, your only way out is to surrender yourself to Jesus. The One who delivered Mary Magdalene is ready to deliver you.

THE BOTTOMLESS PIT

Revelation 9:1-2:

> *And the fifth angel sounded, and I saw a star fall from heaven unto the earth: and to him was given the key of the bottomless pit. And he opened the bottomless pit; and there arose a smoke out of the pit, as the smoke of a great furnace; and the sun and the air were darkened by reason of the smoke of the pit.*

The angel blew his trumpet, a star fell on earth and this star was given the key to the bottomless pit. This cannot be an ordinary star. There are several instances in the Bible where angels are referred to as stars. An example is in Job 38:4 and 7:

> *Where wast thou when I laid the foundations of the earth? declare, if thou hast understanding. When the morning stars sang together, and all the sons of God shouted for joy?*

God is saying here that the morning stars sang together when He laid the foundation of the earth. The morning stars here must be angels.

The bottomless pit is a special place where enemies of God will be kept. It is a prison that God has already prepared for those that He wants to punish. Isaiah 24:21-22 confirms this:

> *And it shall come to pass in that day, that the LORD shall punish the host of the high ones that are on high, and the kings of the earth upon the earth. And they shall be gathered together, as prisoners are gathered in the pit, and shall be shut up in the prison, and after many days shall they be visited.*

It can be compared to putting people in the police cell before taking them to prison. We do not know exactly where this bottomless pit is located but we need not know because we are not going there. There are certain demons being kept in the bottomless pit because they are dangerous to human beings. When this pit is opened, these demonic prisoners will be let loose on the people on earth after some of us must have gone to Heaven.

Let us look at Revelation 9:3-12:

> *And there came out of the smoke locusts upon the earth: and unto them was given power, as the scorpions of the earth have power. And it was commanded them that they should not hurt the grass of the earth, neither any green thing, neither any tree; but only those men which have not the seal of God in their foreheads. And to them it was given that they should not kill them, but that they should be tormented five months: and their torment was as the torment of a scorpion, when he striketh a man. And in those days shall men seek death, and shall not find it; and shall desire to die, and death shall flee from them. And the shapes of the locusts were like unto horses prepared unto battle; and on their heads were as it were crowns like gold, and their faces were as the faces of men. And they had hair as the hair of women, and their teeth were as the teeth of lions. And they had breastplates, as it were breastplates of iron; and the sound of their wings was as the sound of chariots of many horses running to battle. And they had tails like unto scorpions, and there were stings in their tails: and their power was to hurt men five months. And they had a king over them, which is the angel of the bottomless pit, whose name in the Hebrew tongue is Abaddon, but in the Greek tongue hath his name Apollyon. One woe is past; and, behold, there come two woes more hereafter.*

The locust is a symbol of destruction. When locusts hit a farm, by the time they leave, no vegetation is left. The locusts were told not to touch any green thing. They were told to deal with human beings only. Normally, locusts do not attack human beings.

The locusts were told not to kill the people but just to torment them after the manner of scorpions, for five months. Several years ago, the Americans started developing the neutron bomb. The neutron, bomb does not destroy houses or trees. It destroys only human beings. It paralyses human beings.

It is interesting that when we look at the description given to the locusts, we are told that they looked like horses with faces of men. They are described as having hair like that of a woman and breastplates of iron. They made a noise like horses going to battle. This looks like the description of a helicopter as someone saw it many years ago.

The American miliary use a type of helicopter called the Cobra. At the base of these helicopters is painted a picture of a lion with its teeth wide open. I am sure that these were the helicopters that John saw two thousand years ago. He must have seen the faces of the pilots and thought that they were the faces of the helicopters. He saw bombs drop from their tails. God does not have to do anything further in respect of the things that He said would happen. All He has to do is to fold His arms because the scientists are already producing the devices that will be used during the period of the tribulation.

You may wonder why these locusts came from the ground. Since the Second World War, the superpowers have stored most of their weapons underground. A day will come when God will open the doors and these helicopters will rise up into action, dropping neutron bombs. Those who inhale the resulting fumes will beg God to kill them when the pain becomes unbearable. Mighty men of valour will weep but they will not die. This will last for five months. Thank God, I will not be around when this happens.

Jeremiah 8:3 tells us about a day when those who are dead will be more fortunate than those alive:

And death shall be chosen rather than life by all the residue of them that remain of this evil family, which remain in all the places whither I have driven them, saith the LORD of hosts.

THE DEMONS IN THE RIVER EUPHRATES

Revelation 9:13-21:

And the sixth angel sounded, and I heard a voice from the four horns of the golden altar which is before God, saying to the sixth angel which had the trumpet, Loose the four angels which are bound in the great river Euphrates. And the four angels were loosed, which were prepared for an hour, and a day, and a month, and a year, for to slay the third part of men. And the number of the army of the horsemen were two hundred thousand thousand: and I heard the number of them. And thus I saw the horses in the vision, and them that sat on them, having breastplates of fire, and of jacinth, and brimstone: and the heads of the horses were as the heads of lions; and out of their mouths issued fire and smoke and brimstone. By these three was the third part of men killed, by the fire, and by the smoke, and by the brimstone, which issued out of their mouths. For their power is in their mouth, and in their tails: for their tails were like unto serpents, and had heads, and with them they do hurt. And the rest of the men which were not killed by these plagues yet repented not of the works of their hands, that they should not worship devils, and idols of gold, and silver, and brass, and stone, and of wood: which neither can see, nor hear, nor walk: Neither repented they of their murders, nor of their sorceries, nor of their fornication, nor of their thefts.

An interesting thing is that during the first terrible five months nobody asks for forgiveness from God. All that they wanted was that God should kill them. Since they did not repent, the punishment had to continue.

The sixth angel sounded his trumpet and he was told to release the four angels bound at the river Euphrates. The river flowed through the Garden of Eden. It is believed by Bible scholars that the original headquarters of Satan was on the bank of this river. It was from there that Satan went to tempt Eve. Bible scholars have also found out that Cain killed Abel beside this river. Also, during the building of the tower of Babel, water was drawn from this river to make blocks. The tower of Babel was built by the bank of the river Euphrates.

According to John, God has a special prison house built near this river. In the prison are four dangerous angels found with chains. These angels will be freed at a particular year, a particular month, day and a particular hour. When they are let loose, they will gather two hundred million soldiers, and will give them power to destroy one third of the world's population. Two thousand years ago when John wrote this, the population of the earth had not reached two hundred million.

However, on April 24 1964, a certain expert in defence, writing about the Chinese, said that if there were to be a nuclear war many people may die but there would be enough Chinese alive. By 1964 the Chinese army numbered 200 million. Everything that God has mentioned is ready. What these angels will do is just to move over to China and tell them to face the rest of the world in battle.

The river Euphrates is the boundary between the east and the West. The angels will go to the east to recruit their army.

John was not really able to find the right words to describe these 'horses'. They were made of iron and fire was coming out of their mouths. John used the language available to him to describe what he saw. There will be 200 million armoured cars rolling out of China to perpetuate destruction.

Where will they find one-third of the world to destroy? They probably have to go to India. The population of India today is close to one billion. This is about a quarter of the total world population. In India today, there are more than 30 million idols. In fact, if you talk about Jesus to them, they will tell you that they would like to include Him as one of their idols.

The remaining two-thirds, according to the Bible, will still not repent. They will continue with idol worship. Today, for example, we have the Church of

Satan in California, U.S.A They have their own ten commandments, which are the exact opposite of the ten commandments from God. On their altar, during their services, a naked woman is always placed and fornication is the order of the day. In America and Europe, witches now hold conventions and some of these are even televised.

Revelation 9:21 tells us the four great sins that will end the world. They are murder, sorcery, fornication and theft. Today, murder has become rampant. People are murdered every day and nobody pays attention anymore. Sorcery, in the original version of the Bible, is witchcraft with the use of drugs. Some few years ago, cocaine was not a common drug, but now it is used all over the world.

Fornication is not new either. We now have group sex, wife-swopping, homosexuality and lesbianism. These groups hold protest marches in America. Nudists' camps are commonplace; In some universities, girls hold competitions to see who can walk naked the farthest before being arrested. Stealing is no longer a rare occurrence. In earlier centuries, thieves robbed at night with fear but nowadays they rob in the daytime and even tell you that they are coming.

All this is written to indicate us three important things. First, there is no religion that foretells the future in the manner which Christianity does. Second, the things that are happening now are to warn the world that the end is near. Third, you have to be born again, or very soon, you will not be able to be saved. When the salt of the world has been removed, the destruction that will follow will be very terrible.

For those of us who are already born again, this chapter points to the fact that our Bridegroom will soon come. We should hold fast because the day of our redemption draws near. It would be a tragedy for a born again Christian to backslide and partake of the tribulation.

Chapter 20

THE JOYS AND SORROWS OF A PROPHET

Revelation 10:1-4

> *And I saw another mighty angel come down from heaven, clothed with a cloud: and a rainbow was upon his head, and his face was as it were the sun, and his feet as pillars of fire: And he had in his hand a little book open: and he set his right foot upon the sea, and his left foot on the earth, And cried with a loud voice, as when a lion roareth: and when he had cried, seven thunders uttered their voices. And when the seven thunders had uttered their voices, I was about to write: and I heard a voice from heaven saying unto me, Seal up those things which the seven thunders uttered, and write them not.*

The seventh angel was yet to sound His trumpet. There was a kind of interlude between the sixth and seventh trumpet. We are taken from earth to the spiritual realm to see certain things happen. John saw another mighty angel clothed in clouds. The clouds are the chariots of God. Psalm 104:1 and 3:

> *Bless the LORD, O my soul. O LORD my God, thou art very great; thou art clothed with honour and majesty. Who layeth the beams of his chambers in the waters: who maketh the clouds his chariot: who walketh upon the wings of the wind:*

This mighty angel had a rainbow on his head. Let us read from Ezekiel 1:28 what the Bible says about the rainbow:

> *As the appearance of the bow that is in the cloud in the day of rain, so was the appearance of the brightness round about. This was the appearance of the likeness of the glory of the LORD. And when I saw it, I fell upon my face, and I heard a voice of one that spake.*

This is the likeness of the glory of God. The Lord makes the clouds His chariot and this being with the rainbow around his head, from what we have read in the book of Ezekiel, might be the Lord. We will find out later.

John said his face was as the sun. Matthew 17:1-2 says:

> *And after six days Jesus taketh Peter, James, and John his brother, and bringeth them up into an high mountain apart, And was transfigured before them: and his face did shine as the sun, and his raiment was white as the light.*

Also, who is the person with his feet as pillars of fire? Revelation 1:15 gives a clue:

> *And his feet like unto fine brass, as if they burned in a furnace; and his voice as the sound of many waters.*

By now we should have an idea of who this mighty angel might be. In Revelation 10:3 we are told that he cried with a loud voice as when a lion roars. Let us compare this with Joel 3:16:

> *The LORD also shall roar out of Zion, and utter his voice from Jerusalem; and the heavens and the earth shall shake: but the LORD will be the hope of his people, and the strength of the children of Israel.*

The Last Days

The argument is conclusive. The mighty angel was none other than the glorified Christ. Revelation 10:2 says that his right foot was on the sea and the left foot on the earth. Bible scholars also believe, that this points to the glorified Christ. As big as angels are, they are not as big as God; Also; the Bible. tells us that God uses the earth as His footstool (Matthew 5:35).

When the angel cried, seven thunders tittered their voice. What were these seven voices? They are the voices of God. Psalm 29:3-5.

> *The voice of the LORD is upon the waters: the God of glory thundereth: the LORD is upon many waters. The voice of the LORD is powerful; the voice of the LORD is full of majesty. The voice of the LORD breaketh the cedars; yea, the LORD breaketh the cedars of Lebanon.*

Psalm 29:7-9:

> *The voice of the LORD divideth the flames of fire, The voice of the LORD shaketh the wilderness; the LORD shaketh the wilderness of Kadesh. The voice of the LORD maketh the hinds to calve, and discovereth the forests: and in his temple doth everyone speak of his glory.*

In Revelation 10:4 when the seven thunders uttered their voices, John was about to write, but a voice told him not to write. At the beginning of the Book of Revelation, Jesus told John that he must write everything that he saw and heard. However, at this stage he was told not to write.

He was told not to write because there is certain information meant for prophets only. This could be for several reasons. It could be because the people he was speaking to were not ready for the message. When people go to a man of God for assistance, from the way they talk, you know what they are ready to receive and what they are not ready for.

In 2 Corinthians 12:2 and 4, Paul said:

> *I knew a man in Christ above fourteen years ago, (whether in the body, I cannot tell; or whether out of the body, I cannot tell: God knoweth;)*

such an one caught up to the third heaven. How that he was caught up into paradise, and heard unspeakable words, which it is not lawful for a man to utter.

There are certain things that you hear that you cannot tell others. Even Jesus could not tell His disciples everything. If God tells a prophet that a certain person will die, do you think the prophet will tell the person? This is part of the joys and sorrows of a prophet.

Chapter 21

THE ANTICHRIST

Revelation 10:5-7:

> *And the angel which I saw stand upon the sea and upon the earth lifted up his hand to heaven, And sware by him that liveth for ever and ever, who created heaven, and the things that therein are, and the earth, and the things that therein are, and the sea, and the things which are therein, that there should be time no longer: But in the days of the voice of the seventh angel, when he shall begin to sound, the mystery of God should be finished, as he hath declared to his servants the prophets.*

This mighty angel said that time shall be no more. This means that the end has come. Hebrews 10:36-37 refers to this particular time which the angel was talking about:

> *For ye have need of patience, that, after ye have done the will of God, ye might receive the promise. For yet a little while, and he that shall come will come, and will not tarry.*

Who is this one that will come? He is Jesus Christ. However, before Jesus comes, the Antichrist would have come. Before Jesus comes to reign for a thousand years, the Antichrist will come to reign for seven years.

In Revelation 10:8-11, we are, introduced to a book, opening:

> *And the voice which I heard from heaven spake unto me again, and said, Go and take the little book which is open in the hand of the angel which standeth upon the sea and upon the earth. And I went unto the angel, and said unto him, Give me the little book. And he said unto me, Take it, and eat it up; and it shall make thy belly bitter, but it shall be in thy mouth sweet as honey. And I took the little book out of the angel's hand, and ate it up; and it was in my mouth sweet as honey: and as soon as I had eaten it, my belly was bitter. And he said unto me, Thou must prophesy again before many peoples, and nations, and tongues, and kings.*

What is this little book? We do not know for sure. We do not have enough Bible references about the little book. We will discover when we get to Heaven.

The voice from Heaven asked John to go and take the book. When he got to the angel and asked for it, the angel said he should take it. Any revelation from God will not be forced on you. You will have to take it yourself. John was told to eat the book. Some Bible scholars believe that the little book is the sum total of the word of God. Jesus said that we must eat His body (Matthew 26:26): Jesus is the Word of God. In the past, people referred to the word of God as sweeter than honey.

In another place Jesus said He is the Bread of life and that we must eat Him if we want to live for ever (John 6:51). What do we mean by eating the word of God? There are people who read the Bible as we read a novel. There are others who study the Bible in detail, while some memorise it.

After John ate the book, certain information became available to him.

The Last Days

When he got the entire information, he became very despondent. Initially he was happy but when he saw the things that God wanted to do, he became very sad. He saw a glimpse of what the Antichrist would do.

Who exactly is the Antichrist? For what does he stand? Before the period of the New Testament, the idea of a certain force opposed to God had always been there. In the scriptures, we read about the serpent, the dragon and so on. However, a name keeps on recurring in the Old Testament. That name is Belial.

In the Bible, whenever someone was evil, he was called a descendant of Belial. The sons of Eli were called sons of Belial in 1 Samuel 2:12. Hannah thought she was being called a daughter of Belial in 1 Samuel 1:16 when the priest assumed that she was drunk. Jezebel persuaded sons of Belial to lie against Naboth in 1 Kings 21:13. The name also crops up in the New Testament in 2 Corinthians 6:15.

Later on, Belial's name was changed to Antichrist. Paul told us in 2 Corinthians 11:13-15 about the plan of the devil to produce his own masterpiece, just as God produced Jesus. Satan wants to produce his own begotten son who will have all the characteristics of the Devil. Satan has been working on this for some time now but Someone has been preventing him from achieving his goal. 2 Thessalonians 2:7 says:

> *For the mystery of iniquity doth already work: only he who now letteth will let, until he be taken out of the way.*

The Holy Spirit has been preventing Satan from achieving his goal. Right now, the Holy Spirit is gathering those who belong to God. As soon as the total number that God has determined is complete, the trumpet will sound in Heaven and the Holy Spirit will take this number away from the earth. As soon as the Holy Spirit has completed this task, the Devil will be free to produce his own son.

The time of the Antichrist will be a terrible one. The laws at the time will be like those of the church of Satan in California. It will be a matter of live and let die. People will be promoted for killing their parents. The more wicked you are, the better for you. This period will happen for seven years.

How do we recognise the spirit of the Antichrist? 1 John 2:22

> *Who is a liar but he that denieth that Jesus is the Christ? He is antichrist, that denieth the Father and the Son.*

The Antichrist is the one who says that God has no son. Also, 1 John 4:3 says:

> *And every spirit that confesseth not that Jesus Christ is come in the flesh is not of God: and this is that spirit of antichrist, whereof ye have heard that it should come; and even now already is it in the world.*

Those with the spirit of the Antichrist say that Jesus will come again as a spirit. Some even say that He has come already and that nobody saw Him. One way by which you can know whether an angel or a prophet is from God is by asking whether Jesus has come in the flesh or not. If the answer is negative you can be sure that he is from the Devil.

The Antichrist is coming, whether we like it or not. When he comes, there will be no one to restrain him. The Holy Spirit would have gone. The Church that is the salt of the earth would have gone and everything would have turned sour.

The Antichrist will announce that he is the only begotten son of the Devil and that he must be worshiped. To be left behind to face such a situation is the worst thing that can happen to anybody.

Chapter 22

THE TRUE TEMPLES OF CHRIST

Revelation 11:1-2:

And there was given me a reed like unto a rod: and the angel stood, saying, Rise, and measure the temple of God, and the altar, and them that worship therein. But the court which is without the temple leave out, and measure it not; for it is given unto the Gentiles: and the holy city shall they tread under foot forty and two months.

Revelation Chapter 11 makes an interesting study indeed. John was given a measuring instrument and he was told to measure the temple of God, the altar and those that worshipped therein. We have to first find out which temple he was told to measure.

The temple of Christ's days, that is the temple of Herod, had already been levelled by Titus when he led the Roman legions against the Jews twenty-five years before the Book of Revelation was written. As a matter of fact, some Bible scholars believe fervently that there is going to be a new temple built some three and a half years after the Antichrist is first revealed. The

Jews would build this temple and the one to assist in its building is the Antichrist himself. This notion is confirmed in Daniel 9:27:

> *I shall confirm the covenant with many for one week: and in midst of the week he shall cause the sacrifice and the oblation to cease, and for the overspreading of abominations he shall make desolate, even until the consummation, and that determined shall be poured upon the desolate.*

The Antichrist will enable the Jews to begin to worship God the way they did before AD70. That is, by offering sacrifices in the temple.

Where will this temple be located? There is a place in Jerusalem called the mosque of Omar. This mosque is located right on the spot where the old temple was situated. The Jews were kept away from the temple site from AD70 until the six-day war of 1967 when they recaptured the old city wall of Jerusalem.

Since this time, archaeologists have started excavating in Jerusalem and one of the things they have discovered is one of the pillars of Solomon's temple. By their calculating from the location of this pillar they have located where the Holy of Holies of the temple was located. It is right under the mosque of Omar. How will this temple be rebuilt? The only way would be to destroy the mosque, which seems impossible because the mosque is the second holiest place for Moslems after Mecca. An earthquake will have to do the levelling of the mosque.

Any time from now, the Lord will come and once He arrives there will be all kinds of earthquakes. The Jews will rebuild their temple. When the Antichrist comes, he will allow the Jews to build their temple in exchange for their support. After three and a half years, he will break his covenant with them and tell them that he is the real God. He will put himself in the temple and insist that he must be worshipped. He will offer swine on the altar. This is the greatest blasphemy anyone can commit against God in the eyes of the Jews.

John was asked to measure the temple, the altar and the people therein. Measuring the temple does not sound strange, neither does measuring the altar. However, what is the meaning of measuring the people therein? Any time that God wants to evaluate his people, He uses the word, 'measure'. God is constantly asking that we examine ourselves. This is necessary because things are not always what they appear to be on the surface. It will be good for Christians constantly to measure themselves so as to know whether they are backsliding or not.

There was once a temple in Jerusalem. There will be another temple in the future. Today, there are temples of the Most High, but they are not built with hands. I am one of them. What about you? 1 Peter 2:5 says:

Ye also, as lively stones, are built up a spiritual house, an holy priesthood, to offer up spiritual sacrifices, acceptable to God by Jesus Christ.

Today, when God wants to build a temple, He does not use blocks and bricks. He uses Christians as stones. Ephesians 2:19-21 says:

Now therefore ye are no more strangers and foreigners, but fellow citizens with the saints, and of the household of God; And are built upon the foundation of the apostles and prophets, Jesus Christ himself being the chief corner stone; In whom all the building fitly framed together groweth unto an holy temple in the Lord.

The temple of the Almighty God today has the apostles and the prophets as the foundation, Jesus as the cornerstone and us as the living stones built on them. We have to ensure the temple keeps growing day by day. This is more clearly stated in 1 Corinthians 3:16:

Know ye not that ye are the temple of God, and that the Spirit of God dwelleth in you?

We are the temple of God and the Spirit of God dwells in us. God wants to determine our spiritual weight. How much we weigh is determined by several factors. This includes our faith and trust in Him. For example, David faced Goliath in the Name of the Lord while Saul and the priests shied away. David became a man after God's heart because he trusted God. Another example is the sequence of events in Luke 1 which began when God sent an angel to Zacharias. He was told that his wife would conceive and he asked for a sign (Luke 1:18). He went dumb. When the same angel went to the Virgin Mary and told her that she was going to be conceived by the Holy Ghost, she did not argue (Luke 1:38). Spiritually, Mary weighed more than Zacharias the priest.

If God were to weigh you today, how heavy would you be spiritually? Many of us trust in the people that we know and not in God. The degree to which you fellowship with sinners will also determine your weight. 2 Corinthians 6:16-17 says:

> *And what agreement hath the temple of God with idols? For ye are the temple of the living God; as God hath said, I will dwell in them, and walk in them; and I will be their God, and they shall be my people. Wherefore come out from among them, and be ye separate, saith the Lord, and touch not the unclean thing; and I will receive you.*

What this means is that you should not do the things sinners do. There are many Christians today who make excuses for their behaviour. If you want to please the world, you are going to weigh very little with God. The Bible says that friendship with the world is enmity with God. I will rather be a friend of God than a friend of the world.

If the whole world is against you but God is with you, then rejoice. However, if the world loves you but God hates you, beware. If the world fights against you, you can appeal to the Almighty God. The Bible says that if God be for us, who can be against us? (Romans 8:31). However, if God is against you, who can be for you?

Chapter 23

THE TWO WITNESSES

Revelation 11:3-6:

> *And I will give power unto my two witnesses, and they shall prophesy a thousand two hundred and threescore days, clothed in sackcloth. These are the two olive trees, and the two candlesticks standing before the God of the earth. And if any man will hurt them, fire proceedeth out of their mouth, and devoureth their enemies: and if any man will hurt them, he must in this manner be killed. These have power to shut heaven, that it rain not in the days of their prophecy: and have power over waters to turn them to blood, and to smite the earth with all plagues, as often as they will.*

We are here introduced to two witnesses. At the time of the tribulation, God is going to send two remarkable evangelists. They will arrive at the same time as the Antichrist. They will tell the Jews that their sacrifices in the new temple are no longer necessary because Jesus had already finished all sacrifices by His death on the cross. They will let the Jews know that the real

Messiah has already come and gone, to come back later. The Jews will hate these evangelists. The evangelists will make the Jews understand that the Antichrist is not their friend but their number one enemy and that he is the child of the Devil and a beast.

The Antichrist will not like this at all. Today, anyone who preaches holiness is not liked. The popular pastors of today are the ones who preach prosperity alone. Anyone who preaches the whole truth and nothing but the truth is not often popular. However, truth will always prevail.

I used to have many friends abroad until I began to talk to them about sanctification, self-denial, making sacrifices for Christ and living a crucified life. They could not cope so they looked around for people who would tell them they could do whatever they liked because they are in the period of grace. Very soon, He who will come will come. The word of God will always be true. Broad is the way that leads to eternal perdition and many will walk on it. Narrow and straight is the other way and very few people will walk on it.

The Antichrist will kill the two witnesses after three and a half years. The witnesses will not be killed until they have finished their mission. During these three and a half years, they will destroy their enemies with fire from their mouths.

Who are these two witnesses? There have been a lot of arguments about who they are. Many theologians believe that one of them will be Elijah. There are those who say the second witness will be Enoch. This is because they were the only two people who never tasted death. The scriptures say that it is appointed to man once to die, but Elijah and Enoch were taken up so they will have to come back to keep their appointments with death .

A closer study of the scriptures, however, shows clearly that they are not Elijah and Enoch but Elijah and Moses. Malachi 3 confirms this, as does Malachi 4:5-6 which says:

> *Behold, I will send you Elijah the prophet before the coming of the great and dreadful day of the LORD: And he shall turn the heart of the fathers to the children, and the heart of the children to their fathers, lest I come and smite the earth with a curse.*

There are other passages in the Bible to support this claim:

1 Kings 17:1

> *And Elijah the Tishbite, who was of the inhabitants of Gilead, said unto Ahab,, As the LORD God of Israel liveth, before whom I stand, there shall not be dew nor rain these years, but according to my word.*

2 Kings 1:9-10:

> *Then the king sent unto him a captain of fifty with his fifty. And he went up to him: and, behold, he sat on the top of an hill. And he spake unto him, Thou man of God, the king hath said, Come down. And Elijah answered and said to the captain of fifty, If I be a man of God, then let fire come down from heaven, and consume thee and thy fifty. And there came down fire from heaven, and consumed him and his fifty.*

Mark 9:4:

> *And there appeared unto them Elias with Moses, and they were talking with Jesus.*

Exodus 7:14-18:

> *LORD said unto Moses, Pharaoh's heart is hardened, he refuseth to let the people go. Get thee unto Pharaoh in the morning; lo, he goeth out unto the water; and thou shalt stand by the river's brink against he come; and the rod which was turned to a serpent shalt thou take in thine hand. And thou shalt say unto him, The LORD God of the Hebrews hath sent me unto thee, saying, Let my people go, that they may serve me in the wilderness: and, behold, hitherto thou wouldest not hear. Thus saith the LORD, In this thou shall know that I am the LORD: behold,*

> I will smite with the rod that is in mine hand upon the waters which are in the river; and they shall be turned to blood. And the fish that is in the river shall die, and the river shall stink; and the Egyptians shall lothe to drink of the water of the river.

Numbers 20:12:

> And the LORD spake unto Moses and Aaron, Because ye believed me not, to sanctify me in the eyes of the children of Israel, therefore ye shall not bring this congregation into the land which I have given them.

Moses did not finish his ministry before he died. Likewise Elijah: 2 Kings 2:11:

> And it came to pass, as they still went on, and talked, that, behold, there appeared a chariot of fire, and horses of fire, and parted them both asunder; and Elijah went up by a whirlwind into heaven.

Elijah was removed before he completed his ministry. There are several other proofs in the Bible to show that these witnesses will be Elijah and Moses. For example, they were the two people who spoke to the Lord on the Mount of Transfiguration. Some Bible scholars suggest that they were the two people who appeared to the women at the tomb after Jesus rose from the dead (Mark 16:5), and that they were the two people who spoke to the disciples after Jesus ascended into Heaven. Each time they appeared they were clothed in white and were always together. They were strong, tough, full of faith and were on fire for the Lord.

The important thing, however, is that during the three and a half years of their assignment, nobody was able to kill them. As soon as they finished their assignment, the Antichrist was able to overcome them. One lesson here is that if you are a true child of God, you cannot die until you have finished your mission for God here on earth. It is impossible for you to die until God has finished with you.

Also, a true child of God should not fear death. Death is nothing but a horse to ride into glory. The day you die is the day you are going to be rewarded for all your efforts because after death comes judgement. If you are a true child of God, you have already passed from death into life and there will be no condemnation for you. The only judgement for you is the judgement of reward.

Revelation 11:7-19

> *And when they shall have finished their testimony, the beast that ascendeth out of the bottomless pit shall make war against them, and shall overcome them, and kill them. And their dead bodies shall lie in the street of the great city, which spiritually is called Sodom and Egypt, where also our Lord was crucified. And they of the people and kindreds and tongues and nations shall see their dead bodies three days and an half, and shall not suffer their dead bodies to be put in graves. And they that dwell upon the earth shall rejoice over them, and make merry, and shall send gifts one to another; because these two prophets tormented them that dwelt on the earth. And after three days and an half the Spirit of life from God entered into them, and they stood upon their feet; and great fear fell upon them which saw them. And they heard a great voice from heaven saying unto them, Come up hither. And they ascended up to heaven in a cloud; and their enemies beheld them. And the same hour was there a great earthquake, and the tenth part of the city fell, and in the earthquake were slain of men seven thousand: and the remnant were affrighted, and gave glory to the God of heaven. The second woe is past; and, behold, the third woe cometh quickly. And the seventh angel sounded; and there were great voices in heaven, saying, The kingdoms of this world are become the kingdoms of our Lord, and of his Christ; and he shall reign for ever and ever. And the four and twenty elders, which sat before God on their seats, fell upon their faces, and worshipped God, Saying, We give thee thanks, O Lord God Almighty, which art, and wast, and art to come; because thou hast taken to thee thy great power, and hast reigned. And the nations were angry,*

The Last Days

and thy wrath is come, and the time of the dead, that thy should be judged, and that thou shouldest give reward unto they servants the prophets, and to the saints, and them that fear thy name, small and great; and shouldest destroy them which destroy the earth. And the temple of God was opened in heaven, and there was seen in his temple the ark of his testament: and there were lightnings, and voices, and thunderings, and an earthquake, and great hail.

When the Antichrist kills the two witnesses, the whole world will rejoice. There will be a kind of satanic jubilation. There will be an exchange of gifts and great merriment because of the demise of these two men. One question that had been a bother to bible scholars for many years was how the whole world will be able to see these two witnesses, at the same time as they will be lying in Jerusalem. This problem has been solved a long time ago. They will be seen via satellite. The whole world will watch them for three and a half days, via satellite. While still being watched, life will come into them and they will ascend to Heaven. A lesson to learn from this is that Satan's triumphs are always short-lived. God always has the last laugh. The Bible is full of examples and few of them are worth looking at.

During the episode of the crossing of the Red Sea, I am sure that the Devil must have been rejoicing when the Israelites reached the Red Sea and could go no further. The greatest desire of the Devil was to wipe out the Israelites because he knew that the Saviour would come from that race. However, all his plans failed.

There may be some of us who think that we are at the end of the road and that the end has come. If you are fully on the Lord's side, there will always be a way forward for you. You may not know it yet but that will surely happen because God always has the last word.

There is also the story of Joshua and the defeat at Ai (Joshua 7). After the great victory at Jericho, Satan moved upon Achan and told him to disobey God. God told the Israelites not to take any of the treasures in Jericho for themselves but Achan stole some treasures and buried them in his tent. The children of Israel went to battle and fled before their enemies. At this time they were newly arrived in the Promised Land and they still had memories of their slavery in Egypt. The defeat at Ai was a crushing blow to Joshua, the young leader, who had just taken over from Moses. He fell on his face and began to seek the face of the Lord.

God told Joshua what to do to the man that had sinned and added that they all should make restitution. They did this and victory was so complete that all the neighbouring kings heard about it. Joshua never suffered any further defeats, right up to the time of his death. I believe that some of us have been defeated because sin has entered into our camp. We did not check ourselves thoroughly because we had become cold, without knowing it. If we put things right. God will give us the final victory.

There is also the account of the capture of Samson (Judges 16). Samson behaved foolishly and because God delayed bringing in His judgement, he kept on going deeper and deeper into sin until finally the enemy overcame him. They put out his two eyes and made him dance in their temple. As far as the Devil was concerned, his victory was complete. However. Samson repented and he got back into communion with God. Even though he died, the Bible tells us that the enemies he killed at his death were more than those he killed in his lifetime.

A lesson to learn from Samson is that he could still have destroyed those people and lived. Samson could have regained his sight if he had asked God for it. Many of us have failed God and we know it. Many times, because of the zeal that comes from repentance, we say prayers that are not right. If you say solemn prayers particularly at the moment of repentance, the answer may come exactly as you want it.

A young man, filled with the spirit and doing exploits for the Lord, fell into fornication; It pained him so much that at the point of repentance, he prayed to God for forgiveness and asked God to remove the power of his manhood from him. For years now, he has been praying for the power to be restored, without any success. God is not interested in your destruction. God has no pleasure in the death of sinners. He wants you to repent and live. He wants the victory that He will give you, when you repent, to be total.

There is also the story of Daniel in the lions' den (Daniel 6). You know how Daniel got into the den and how he got out of it. I am sure that after it became known that Daniel had been thrown into the lions' den, the king had to struggle very hard to get him delivered. Daniel too must have prayed. Even though his prayer was not recorded in the Bible, I am sure that he would have implored God to demonstrate to the people that He is the Almighty God. God allowed Daniel to go into the den and come out untouched and alive. God never says no to any of our prayers. What He may say is that He has a better idea. It is a better idea to go into the lions' den and come out alive than not to go at all. The name of Daniel is immortalised because he went into the den and came out alive.

The same is true of Meshach, Shadrach and Abednego. I am sure that when they were making their positive confession to the king, they were very sure that before they got to the fiery furnace, something would happen to prevent it (Daniel 3). However, nothing happened. They were led into the furnace because God had a better idea. He wanted to teach the king a lesson greater than what Meshach, Shadrach and Abednego could have imagined.

Perhaps you have been praying for something and you have not had the result you desired. Please do not judge God foolishly because of this, thinking He has not heard your prayers or that He is a liar. He may have something far better than that for which you are asking.

The best example to show that God always laughs last is found in the crucifixion of our Lord Jesus Christ. I am sure that when Jesus was praying in the Garden of Gethsemane, He would have thought that God would re

The Last Days

write the story and prevent Him from being crucified (Mark 14:32-35). However, God the Father had a better idea. Because He refused to grant the request of His Son at that time, today at the mention of the Name of Jesus every knee should bow.

Real faith in the Almighty God does not mean that we will get everything that we ask for at the time we ask for it. Real faith is when you leave God to do His perfect will. The Devil may win the battle but it is the Almighty God that wins the war. In every war, there may be many battles but it is not the one who wins a few battles that is important but the one who wins the war.

When the two witnesses rose from the dead, they were taken up to Heaven. All those who were left behind were frightened and gave glory to God. However, the glory that they gave to God was short-lived because they did not repent. Many of us may have always asked God to perform a miracle in our family so that every member would be converted, but they may not get converted because of seeing a miracle.

When they see a miracle, they give glory to God but this does not mean that they will become Christians.

We must take special note of this because many of us have been disappointed in this way. When you ask God to perform a miracle, He may do it because it is written that without signs and wonders people may not believe. It does not automatically follow, however, that people will believe because of a miracle.

In Revelation 11:15-19, the final trumpet was blown and this signalled that the end was near, when both the righteous and the wicked are going to be judged. The Almighty was about to take over the kingdoms of the earth. We must note that the statement in verse 15 was made in the middle of the tribulation, when there were still three and a half years to go before Christ will come and set up His Kingdom which will last for a thousand years. After this one thousand years, Satan, who will be bound throughout this period, will be released for a short time and will trigger another rebellion. Satan will then be finally sent to his resting place.

The date that it was announced that the kingdom on earth had been taken over by Jesus was not the actual day that He took over. There was a gap of three and a half years between the announcements and the actual takeover. Many times, when a word of prophecy comes to us, we expect it to come to pass immediately. Many times, when God says something has been done, you may have to wait for another three and a half years to see the result.

Between the time that God says it is done and the time that you see the manifestation proving that it is done, please do not lose your faith in Him. There are many people who have lost their miracles during the interval of waiting. If God has ever spoken to you that it is done, believe it that it is done. Do not let the Devil steal your miracle from you in the interval of waiting; what you should rather do is to praise God.

Chapter 24

THE WOMAN AND THE CHILD

Revelation 12:1-6:

> And there appeared a great wonder in heaven; a woman clothed with the sun, and the moon under her feet, and upon her head a crown of twelve stars: And she being with child cried, travailing in birth, and pained to be delivered. And there appeared another wonder in heaven; and behold a great red dragon, having seven heads and ten horns, and seven crowns upon his heads. And his tail drew the third part of the stars of heaven, and did cast them to the earth: and the dragon stood before the woman which was ready to be delivered, for to devour her child as soon as it was born. And she brought forth a man child, who was to rule all nations with a rod of iron: and her child was caught up unto God, and to his throne. And the woman fled into the wilderness, where she hath a place prepared of God, that they should feed her there a thousand two hundred and threescore days.

The twelfth chapter is one of the most difficult chapters in the Book of

Revelation. Bible scholars have given many different interpretations of this chapter.

Who was the woman clothed with the sun, with the moon under her feet and with a crown of twelve stars? Who was the man-child to be born? Who was the red dragon ready to swallow the child? Why was the child caught up to Heaven as soon as he was born? Why was the mother left behind? Why did the mother have to run into the wilderness? Who prepared the place to which she ran?

We will answer some of these questions.

The dragon was none other than Satan. He is called many names and one of them is a dragon. The one who was waiting to kill a newly born baby can be nobody else but Satan. The child to be born is no other than Jesus. He is going to rule the nation with a rod of iron. This is confirmed in Psalm 2:7 and 9:

> *I will declare the decree: The LORD hath said unto me, Thou art my Son; this day have I begotten thee. Thou shalt break them with a rod of iron; thou shall dash them in pieces like a potter's vessel.*

Some people say that the one to be born is actually a group of overcomers from out of the present Church. This may not satisfy all the scriptures. From the description, the woman to give birth to the child cannot be the Church, for at this point in time, the Church would have already gone to Heaven. The woman cannot be any other woman but the nation of Israel. God has constantly referred to Israel as His wife. For example Isaiah 54:5 says:

> *For thy Maker is thine husband; the LORD of hosts is his name; and thy Redeemer the Holy One of Israel; The God of the whole earth shall he be called.*

God says that Israel is His wife and we know that His only begotten Son is Jesus, who also came from Israel. The twelve stars in the crown of this woman are believed to be the twelve tribes of Israel.

The dragon was waiting to kill the child. This history of the hatred of Satan for the nation of Israel is a very long one. There is no other nation in the whole world that has suffered more at the hands of Satan than the nation of Israel. Twice they have been thrown out of their land and led into captivity in other lands.

Twice Satan wanted to wipe them out completely. Once was during the time of Esther (Esther 3:9) while Hitler made the second attempt. Hitler said that the Jews were destroying the world's culture. He said that in order to preserve the culture of the world, they must be killed. Hitler wiped out more than six million Jews. Yet, some of them survived and the nation of Israel still stands. Napoleon once called the Israelites the greatest wonder on earth. When God loves you specially, the Devil will especially hate you . If the Devil is constantly waging war against you, rejoice, because this is a sign that you are the beloved of God. This, however is only true if you are a Christian.

There are always evil forces ready to destroy those that God loves. When you are on the side of the Devil, he does not bother you much. You are like a chicken in his cage and he can devour you at any time. Once you escape from him, he will run after you, but if you remain steadfast you will always overcome. God always can and will protect His own and no one can destroy those whom God loves. God loves me, so nobody can destroy me.

You may begin to wonder why Satan is very much against the nation of Israel. The story started in Genesis 3:14-15:

> *And the LORD God said unto the serpent. Because thou hast done this, thou art cursed above all cattle, and above every beast of the field; upon thy belly shalt thou go, and dust shalt thou eat all the days of thy life: And I will put enmity between thee and the woman, and between thy seed and her seed; it shall bruise thy head, and thou shalt bruise his heel.*

God said that there will be constant enmity between the seed of the woman and the seed of Satan and that the seed of the woman will bruise the head of Satan. Satan does not like this at all. When Eve began to produce children and brought forth Cain and Abel, Satan was watching out expecting one of them to try to kill him. A day came when the two of them went to offer sacrifices to God and only the sacrifice of Abel was accepted. The Devil thought that it was Abel who would kill him. Within days, Abel was dead, killed by his brother. The Devil thought there were no more serious threats after this incident.

Many years later, however, suddenly God chose Abraham, so the Devil went after him. Sarah was attacked with barrenness. Before Sarah had a child, the Devil had already planted another son, Ishmael, in the house of Abraham.

Among the children of Israel, Joseph was the favourite. Satan tried to destroy him too but he failed. We should also remember what Satan made Pharaoh do to the Israelites. The attack from Satan went on and on until God found someone close to His heart in David. The Devil then turned his attention on David. A lion was sent to attack him but he killed it. Then David defeated Goliath and God won. It does not matter what the Devil may try, we will be more than victorious. The constant enmity between Satan and the Israelites is not a new one. It started in the Garden of Eden and it will continue till we are seated in the heavenly places.

In our Bible passage, as soon as the child was born, it was snatched to Heaven to sit with His Father on His Throne. Jesus is seated with His Father right now but one day, He is coming back to reign. When He comes to reign, we will reign with Him.

The words, 'caught up' in Revelation 12:5 is also used in 1 Thessalonians 4:17-18:

> *Then we which are alive and remain shall be caught up together with them In the clouds, to meet the Lord In the air: and so shall we ever be with the Lord. Wherefore comfort one another with these words.*

The Last Days

The life of anyone beloved of God, will be marked by a continuous battle with the Devil. Although we will win, the Devil will keep on fighting: If you win a battle today, do not relax because your enemy will not rest. Very soon, we will be caught up to Heaven and the Devil will not be able to reach us again. The war will soon be over .

In our Bible passage, we are told that the woman escaped into the wilderness. I think that what God is saying here is that just before Jesus returns to reign for one thousand years, Israel will be like a woman travailing to give birth. Even though we will be in Heaven, the Jews will be here on earth and the Antichrist is going to cause them serious problems. Jesus warned the Jews about this. He said that when the time comes, they had better flee. Mark 13:14 says:

> *But when ye shall see the abomination of desolation, spoken of by Daniel the prophet, standing where it ought not, (let him that readeth understand,) then let them that be in Judaea flee to the mountains.*

With this child taken to Heaven, Satan's next move is recorded in Revelation 12:7-9:

> *And there was war in heaven: Michael and his angels fought against the dragon; and the dragon fought and his angels, and prevailed not; neither was their place found any more in heaven. And the great dragon was cast out, that old serpent, called the Devil, and Satan, which deceiveth the whole world: he was cast out into the earth, and his angels were cast out with him.*

When Satan discovered that the child had been taken up to Heaven, he gathered his fallen angels together and decided to invade the Kingdom of God. Satan really wanted to fight God but God did not even leave His Throne. Jesus was on His Throne and the Heavenly choir was in attendance. God told the angel Michael to take some angels and wipe out Satan and send him and his fallen angels back to earth.

How it is possible for Satan to go and wage war in Heaven? How did he even get there? You have to know that up till now, Satan is still allowed to go into the presence of God. You can read Job chapters 1 and 2 for confirmation.

After God expelled the Devil to the earth, something happened. Revelation 12:10-12:

> *And I heard a loud voice saying in heaven, Now is come salvation, and strength, and the kingdom of our God, and the power of his Christ: for the accuser of our brethren is cast down, which accused them before our God day and night. And they overcame him by the blood of the Lamb, and by the word of their testimony; and they loved not their lives unto the death. Therefore rejoice, ye heavens, and ye that dwell in them. Woe to the inhabiters of the earth and of the sea for the Devil is come down unto you, having great wrath, because he knoweth that he hath but a short time.*

When the Devil was defeated, he was not able to enter Heaven again. He realised that he was soon to be bound. Since a superior force was too powerful for him, he decided to take revenge on an inferior force. When the Devil is not angry he is still dangerous, but he is quite deadly when he becomes really angry.

We have a few lessons to learn from the victory songs of the martyrs. They were rejoicing because Satan was finally thrown out. First, anyone who chooses to suffer for Christ will be the one who has the greatest victory over Satan. If you have to choose between compromising and suffering for Christ, it is better to suffer for Him because the suffering will only be for a short time. You know the story of Joseph. He refused to sin and was put into prison, but he emerged from his cell to become the ruler in Egypt (Genesis 41).

Second, anyone who is not afraid of death cannot be intimidated by the Devil anymore. Jesus said that if you love your life, you would lose it.

However, if you are willing to lose your life for the sake of Christ, you will find it (Matthew 10:39). As soon as the Devil knows that you are ready to die for the sake of Christ, he will leave you but if you are still afraid of death, Satan will torment you.

The victorious Christian has three main weapons. One is the blood of Jesus. The Bible tells us in 1 John 1:7 that the blood of Jesus cleanses from all sins. How does this become a weapon against Satan? Many a time, when as a Christian you want to pray, the Devil torments you and asks whether you really believe that God will answer. He reminds you of your past sins. At times like this, you can turn to him and tell him that the blood of Jesus cleanses you from all sins.

It is written in Romans 8:1-2 that there is now no condemnation for us, because we are already washed in the blood of Jesus. Anytime that the Devil reminds you of your sins, your weapon against him is to tell him what the word of God says about your sins and the blood of Jesus. You should be bold to face Satan with this fact.

The second weapon is a life that witnesses for Christ – a life of good testimonies. Once you say you are a child of God, you must live like one. People are watching you and they take notice of your attitudes to life. Do not let the Devil have any foothold in your life anymore. The accusers are always around. Do not give them an opportunity to ensnare you.

The third weapon against Satan is faithfulness till death. You must be willing to die for your faith. Hold firm to what you believe, no matter what the Devil thinks. For example, no one can enjoy divine healing unless such a person is ready to die. When God is about to heal you, the Devil will tell you that you are about to die. If you listen to him, your faith will crumble. The Bible says that we should be faithful unto death to receive the crown of life (Revelation 2:10).

Let us now move on to the last section of Revelation chapter 12. Revelation 12:13-17:

And when the dragon saw that he was cast unto the earth, he persecuted the woman which brought forth the man child. And to the woman were given two wings of a great eagle, that she might fly into the wilderness, into her place, where she is nourished for a time, and times, and half a time, from the face of the serpent. And the serpent cast out of his mouth water as a flood after the woman, that he might cause her to be carried away of the flood. And the earth helped the woman, and the earth opened her mouth, and swallowed up the flood which the dragon cast out of his mouth. And the dragon was wroth with the woman, and went to make war with the remnant of her seed, which keep the commandments of God, and have the testimony of Jesus Christ.

This section tells us that when the dragon was sent back into the earth, it pursued the woman in order to persecute her. As he was doing this, the Almighty God provided two wings of a great eagle which carried this woman into safety.

For years, Bible scholars did not understand what the wings of a great eagle meant. We now know that this refers to an aeroplane. At that time, the United States of America will come to the aid of the nation of Israel and will evacuate them with aeroplanes to a place where they can hide.

How do we know this? The eagle is the national symbol of America. Right now, in the Mediterranean, very close to Israel, is the base of the American Sixth Fleet, which is made up of a number of aeroplanes. They say that they are just kept there in case of war but we know that God put them there.

I am conscious of the fact that as we study the newspapers day by day, we will get more information about what the Almighty God is planning to do soon. God is almost ready for the second coming of Jesus. I do not know when it is going to happen but I know that I will go with Him. What about you?

Chapter 25

THE ANTICHRIST IS THE BEAST

Revelation 13:1-10:

> *And I stood upon the sand of the sea, and saw a beast rise up out of the sea, having seven heads and ten horns, and upon his horns ten crowns, and upon his heads the name of blasphemy. And the beast which I saw was like unto a leopard, and his feet were as the feet of a bear, and his mouth as the mouth of a lion: and the dragon gave him his power, and his seat, and great authority. And I saw one of his heads as it were wounded to death; and his deadly wound was healed: and all the world wondered after the beast; And they worshipped the dragon which gave power unto the beast: and they worshipped the beast, saying, who is like unto the beast? who is able to make war with him? And there was given unto him a mouth speaking great things and blasphemies; and power was given unto him to continue forty and two months. And he opened his mouth in blasphemy against God, to blaspheme his name, and his tabernacle, and them that dwell in heaven. And it was given unto him to make war with the saints, and to overcome them: and*

power was given him over all kindreds, and tongues, and nations. And all that dwell upon the earth shall worship him, whose names are not written in the book of life of the Lamb slain from the foundation of the world. If any man have an ear, let him hear. He that leadeth into captivity shall go into captivity: he that killeth with the sword must be killed with the sword. Here is the patience and the faith of the saints.

God made use of images to describe to John who the Antichrist would be. God used images common at that time to portray the Antichrist that would come. In Daniel 7:3-7 it was already revealed to Daniel that there would be four kingdoms; each one represented by a beast. Each is represented by a beast because of their wickedness, fierceness and lack of human compassion. Daniel 7:3-7:

And four great beasts came up from the sea, diverse one from another: The first was like a lion, and had eagle's wings: I beheld till the wings thereof were plucked, and it was lifted up from the earth, and made stand upon the feet as a man, and a man's heart was given to it. And behold another beast, a second, like to a bear, and it raised up itself on one side, and it had three ribs in the mouth of it between the teeth of it: and they said thus unto it, Arise, devour much flesh. After this I beheld, and lo another, like a leopard, which had upon the back of it four wings of a fowl; the beast had also four heads; and dominion was given to it. After this I saw in the night visions, and behold a fourth beast, dreadful and terrible, and strong exceedingly; and it had great iron teeth: it devoured and brake in pieces, and stamped the residue with the feet of it: and it was diverse from all the beasts that were before it; and it had ten horns.

God was trying to tell John that the Antichrist would be a combination of all the four beasts described in the above passage. The four rulers that are represented by these four beasts were truly wicked.

The beast described to John had seven heads. This is another illustration that God gave John. The seven heads stand for the seven emperors that ruled Rome from the time of Augustus. These emperors include Tiberius (A.D. 14-37), Caligula (A.D. 37-41), Claudius (A.D. 41-54) and Nero (A.D. 54-68). The others were Vespasian (A.D. 69-79), Titus (A.D. 79-81) and Domitian (A.D. 81-96)

Apart from Vespasian and Titus who were not too bad, the other emperors were horrible even though there was no overt persecution of Christians by the Roman Empire. The most terrible emperor was Nero who regularly persecuted the Christians. Nero died in A.D. 68 while Vespasian started to rule in A.D. 69. Between the reigns of Nero and Vespasian, three emperors reigned for a total of eighteen months – Galba, Otho and Vitellius. Add on these three, and here are the ten horns of the beast. However, the first seven earlier listed were the most significant.

We are told that this beast had the name of blasphemy on his head. Roman emperors were officially regarded as gods and Domitian in particular took his divinity very seriously insisting on being addressed as 'Our Lord and God'. The Antichrist will also have a name that he will call himself.

The beast came out of the sea. The sea represents humanity. In Revelation 17:15 the Bible has this to says:

> *And he saith unto me, The waters which thou sawest, where the whore sitteth, are peoples, and multitudes, and nations, and tongues.*

The Antichrist will emerge from the people. Some scholars believe that he has already been born – between 1960 and 1962. One of these scholars is the same person who said in 1944 that by 1948, Israel would have become a nation again. This came true. Very soon, the Antichrist will emerge. He may be alive now. When the Antichrist comes, he is going to promise peace to the whole world. He will promise to put everything right. At the moment, things are steadily getting worse. However, the worst is yet to come.

One of the things that shows how it will be to hand over the world to the

Antichrist is the fact that dictators have always arisen in difficult situations. When things are terrible and someone comes along to say he will put things right, it is easy for the people to rally round him.

We are told that one of the heads of the beast seemed to have been wounded and that the wound looked as if healed. This language was very clear to John and to the Christians of that time. When Nero died, there was a rumour that he resurrected and this was used to threaten the Christians at the time. Nero was so wicked that people think he is the Antichrist. This is not true. The Antichrist will be far worse.

Let us look at the life of Nero in detail by firstly considering the life of his father – a very wicked man. He killed one of his friends because the friend said he was satisfied during one of their drinking sprees. He once drove his chariots over a lady who was crawling on the ground. There was a time that he plucked out the eyes of an opponent.

Nero's mother was even worse than his father. She killed several people, including an emperor whom she poisoned. She made sure that Nero became the emperor by killing all the other rivals. When Nero's father heard that she was pregnant with him, he said the baby would be nothing but a child of the Devil.

Nero himself committed so much evil that his notoriety will live for ever. He murdered many people. He married two men. When his closest friend died, he took over his wife, Sabina. When Sabina became pregnant, he was so furious that he kicked her till she died. Nero murdered his mother because he wanted to see the womb in which he grew. Nero was responsible for the great fire of Rome in AD 6 and blamed the Christians for it. He was determined to wipe out Christians from this earth.

THE MARK – 666

Revelation 13:11-18:

> *And I beheld another beast coming up out of the earth; and he had two horns like a lamb, and he spake as a dragon. And he exerciseth all the power of the first beast before him, and causeth the earth and them which dwell therein to worship the first beast, whose deadly wound was healed. And he doeth great wonders, so that he maketh fire come down from heaven on the earth in the sight of men, And deceiveth them that dwell on the earth by the means of those miracles which he had power to do in the sight of the beast; saying to them that dwell on the earth, that they should make an image to the beast, which had the wound by a sword, and did live. 'And he had power to give life unto the image of the beast, that the image of the beast should both speak, and cause that as many as would not worship the image of the beast should be killed. And he causeth all, both small and great, rich and poor, free and bond, to receive a mark in their right hand, or in their foreheads: And that no man might buy or sell, save he that had the mark, or the name of the beast, or the number of his name. Here is wisdom. Let him that hath understanding count the number of the beast: for it is the number of a man; and his number is Six hundred threescore and six.*

Here we are introduced to a third beast. The first was the dragon while the second was the beast with the seven heads. The Devil, in attempt to copy God, wants to establish his own trinity. So we have the Devil as the dragon, Devil the father. The Antichrist is Devil the son while the third beast is Devil the unholy spirit. The three of them will continue to rule the world for a period of seven years and the authority of their rule will be very great especially during the first three and a half years.

Why the third beast will ask people to worship the first beast is clear from a statement in John 16:13-14. A certain assignment has been given to the Holy Spirit which the Devil wants to counterfeit:

Howbeit when he, the Spirit of truth, is come, he will guide you into all truth: for he shall not speak of himself; but whatsoever he shall hear, that shall he speak: and he will shew you things to come. He shall glorify me: for he shall receive of mine, and shall show it unto you.

The image that will be made of the Antichrist will be caused to speak by the second beast. How can an image speak? A little bit of what a computer can do will enlighten you more on this issue.

The mark of the Antichrist will be on the right hand of those who are wealthy while it will go on the forehead of the poor. It will be on the right hand of the rich so that it would be recognised when they use their credit cards, or write cheques. For the poor, they would be recognised by the mark on their foreheads when they want to make cash transactions.

The implications of this mark are many. In times past, slaves wore marks of their owners. If you have the mark of the Antichrist on you it means that you are a slave to him. It means that you belong to him, body, soul and spirit and that there is no way that you can be redeemed.

In some ancient languages, letters were used to represent figures, example, the letter A stood for 100, B stood for 101, C stood for 102 and so on. If we write the name 'Hitler' in this way, we will find something interesting:

H	–	107
I	–	108
T	–	119
L	–	111
E	–	104
R	–	117
Total		666

This tells us that there already, has been a preliminary Antichrist. The main one is still to come. If study the life of the Jews under Hitler, you will be able to have a rough idea of what the life of Christians will be under the

Antichrist. It is going to be unpleasant. Anybody without the mark during the time of the Antichrist will not be able to buy or sell, even if they have the money. It will be a question of receive the mark and eat or refuse the mark and die of hunger.

When will this mark begin to be manifest? Already, some people, because they do not want to be carrying money all about, are working on a device that will enable a special computer to read an invisible number on their heads. The computer will read the invisible number and it will be used to transact business with banks.

Those who say that God is preparing Christians so that when the Antichrist comes they will be able to fight him should re-examine their theology. If you say that God does not want Christians to leave with the rapture and that the rapture will take place after the tribulation has already started, I say, be unto you according to your faith.

All those that will remain during the tribulation will worship the Antichrist. The Antichrist will be empowered to make war against those who are left behind and to overcome them. The people that the Devil can overcome are those whose names are not written in the Book of Life, so if your name is not written in the Book of Life, the Devil can still overpower you. If you are not genuinely born again, the Devil can knock you down anytime, anywhere. But if you are a true believer, no forces of darkness can overcome you. John 10:27-29 says:

> *My sheep hear my voice, and I know them, and they follow me: And I give unto them eternal life; and they shall never perish, neither shall any man pluck them out of my hand. My Father, which gave them me, is greater than all; and no man is able to pluck them out of my Father's hand.*

If you are born again, no force on earth can overcome you. Christianity can never be defeated by force. The Gospel of Jesus cannot be destroyed by the violence of man. Nero was determined to wipe out Christianity, but today.

Christianity is stronger than it has ever been and it will continue to be strong. If you receive the mark of Jesus Christ, the Devil will recognise you as such. If you have the mark of Jesus on you, forces of evil will recognise you as belonging to Jesus. If you say that you have given your life to Jesus and forces of darkness are still pursuing you, you need to re-examine your stand.

When you receive the mark of Jesus, it is abundantly clear to forces on earth and in Heaven that you belong to Him, although there may be persecutions. Jesus did not say that once you become born again life would be easy. He said that in this world we will have tribulations but that He has overcome the world (John 16:33).

All those who made a stand for Jesus at the start of their Christian lives, were persecuted at some time or other. However, tribulations always lead to promotions. Joseph took his stand and resisted the Devil. He was imprisoned but from there he moved to the throne. Shadrach, Meshach and Abednego went to the fiery furnace because they refused to bow down to an Antichrist. When they came out, they were promoted. Daniel also went to the lions' den and came out, promoted.

If you take your stand and you are genuinely born again, no matter the number of times that the Devil may throw you down, you will always land on your feet and in a higher place. Every trial that comes your way will lead to promotion.

Chapter 26

A CHRISTIAN IS ONE WHO FOLLOWS CHRIST

Revelation 14:1-5:

> *And I looked, and, lo, a Lamb stood on the mount Sion, and with him an hundred forty and four thousand, having his Father's name written in their foreheads. And I heard a voice from heaven, as the voice of many waters, and as the voice of a great thunder: and I heard the voice of harpers harping with their harps: And they sung as it were a new song before the throne, and before the four beasts, and the elders: and no man could learn that song but the hundred and forty and four thousand, which were redeemed from the earth. These are they which were not defiled with women; for they are virgins. These are they which follow the Lamb whithersoever he goeth. These were redeemed from among men, being the first fruits unto God and to the Lamb. And in their mouth was found no guile: for they are without fault before the throne of God.*

The 144,000 saints had the name of God on their foreheads. The Antichrist also wants to put his name on the heads of people. In the passage above, we see a struggle for foreheads. This tells us that just as God needs our brains, the Devil too will be happy if we surrender our brains to him. When you are marked with a particular brand, it is first and foremost for identification purposes. In other words, God wants those who belong to Him to be identified with Him. The Devil also wants those who belong to him to be identified with him.

These 144,000 people are called God's virgins. Some Christians have twisted this to mean that those who want to be part of this number must never marry. We need to note from such passages as 1 Corinthians 7:2-5, that it is clear that marriage is no sin, if it is done properly. God is not going to reject you simply because you are married.

In 1 Corinthians 7:1 and 7-9, it is clear that those who do not marry are likely to be better than those who marry. If you are not married, it is likely that you will be able to devote yourself to God's work. If you are married, however, your attention will be divided. Nonetheless, if you are married it does not mean that you will be locked out of Heaven.

These 144,000, according to what John saw, followed Christ wherever He went. What we want to point out here is that the simplest definition of a Christian is one who follows Christ. To follow Christ means doing exactly what He does and trying to become like Him. Jesus frequently told His disciples to follow Him (John 1:43, Mark 2:14, Mark 10:21, John 21:19-22). The Bible says in 1 Peter 2:21:

> *For even hereunto were ye called: because Christ also suffered for us, leaving us an example, that ye should follow his steps:*

If you are not following Christ and you say you are a Christian, you are deceiving yourself.

These 144,000 people were called the firstfruits unto the Lamb. The firstfruit is a sacrifice. When you gather in the harvest, you are supposed to bring the firstfruits to God. So, for anyone who wants to qualify to be part of this special people, they must make themselves a living sacrifice to God. Romans 12:1-2:

> I beseech you therefore, brethren, by the mercies of God, that ye present your bodies a living sacrifice, holy, acceptable unto God, which is your reasonable service. And be not conformed to this world: but be ye transformed by the renewing of your mind, that ye may prove what is that good, and acceptable, and perfect, will of God.

There are several ways by which you can make sacrifices to God. For example, you can worship Him with your money. At times, you must give when it is difficult to do so. This is when it becomes a sacrifice.

You can praise Him when praising is very difficult. The Bible says that we should offer sacrifices of praise (Hebrews 13:15). None of us will deny the fact that it is easier, for the natural man, to live in sin than to live in holiness. It is much easier, for example, to yield to temptation than to resist it. To resist temptation and to live a holy life is to live a life of sacrifice. Daily, there are temptations trying to draw you away from Almighty God so daily, you have to resist the flesh and the Devil. The test of your holiness is the number of temptations that you overcome. Temptation is no sin. However, falling into temptation is a sin.

The 144,000 people, we are told, had no guile in their mouths. This means that they never lied. This is enough to disqualify all of us. In Zephaniah 3:13, the Bible says:

> The remnant of Israel shall not do iniquity, nor speak lies; neither shall a deceitful tongue be found in their mouth: for they shall feed and lie down, and none shall make them afraid.

This should make us wake up as far as telling lies is concerned. Many of us consider lying as a very trivial matter. It is, however, a serious matter. Exaggerations are also lies.

The 144,000 people were without blemish. We already know that Christ is coming back for a bride without spot or wrinkle. In Ephesians 1:4, the Bible says:

> *According as he hath chosen us in him before the foundation of the world, that we should be holy and without blame before him in love.*

Ephesians 5:27 adds:

> *That he might present it to himself a glorious church, not having spot, or wrinkle, or any such thing; but that it should be holy and without blemish.*

Matthew 5:48:

> *Be ye therefore perfect, even as your Father which is in heaven is perfect.*

Let us move to the second part of Revelation 14:6-12:

> *And I saw another angel fly in the midst of heaven, having the everlasting gospel to preach unto them that dwell on the earth, and to every nation, and kindred, and tongue, and people, Saying with a loud voice, Fear God, and give glory to him; for the hour of his judgment is come: and worship him that made heaven, and earth, and the sea, and the fountains of waters. And there followed another angel, saying, Babylon is fallen, is fallen, that great city, because she made all nations drink of the wine of the wrath of her fornication. And the third angel followed them, saying with a loud voice, If any man worship the beast and his image, and receive his mark in his forehead, or in his hand, The same shall drink of the wine of the wrath of God, which is poured out without mixture into the cup of his indignation; and he shall be tormented with fire and brimstone in the presence of the holy angels, and in the presence of the Lamb: And the smoke of their torment ascendeth up for ever and ever: and they have no rest day nor night, who worship the beast and his image, and whosoever receiveth the mark of his name. Here is the patience of the saints: here are they that keep the commandments of God, and the faith of Jesus.*

We are introduced to another angel, preaching the Gospel. You may well remember that when God wanted to bring salvation to the house of Cornelius, He sent an angel to him who told him to send for Peter. Why did the angel not go directly to preach salvation to Cornelius? It is because between the day of Pentecost and the rapture, the Almighty God has given us a great opportunity to preach the Gospel of Jesus Christ. If we fail, it will be a loss of great opportunity.

The fact that an angel was preaching is another evidence that those of us who really belong to Jesus will not go through the tribulation. With us having gone, there will be nobody around to witness. The Christians left behind will be so busy hiding from the Antichrist that they will not have time to witness to anyone.

Yet, the Bible says that the whole world must hear the Gospel before the end comes. The Almighty therefore has to take emergency action by sending an angel to fly round the world preaching the Gospel to the world. Everybody will hear the Gospel but whether they will accept it or not is another thing. At least, they will hear before the end comes.

Meanwhile, another angel announced the fall of Babylon. The Babylon that fell was the city of Rome and inside it a lot of things were happening, making people to stumble. The angel announced that Rome would fall just as Sodom and Gomorrah fell. It will be a time of sudden destruction. Several passages in the Bible support this claim:

Isaiah 21:9:

> *And, behold, here cometh a chariot of men, with a couple of horsemen. And he answered and said, Babylon is fallen, is fallen; and all the graven images of her gods he hath broken unto the ground.*

Jeremiah 51:8:

> *Babylon is suddenly fallen and destroyed: howl for her; take balm for her pain, if so be she may be healed.*

Jeremiah 51:7:

> *Babylon hath been a golden cup in the LORD'S hand, that made all the earth drunken: the nations have drunken of her wine; therefore the nations are mad.*

The third angel talked about the doom of those who accepted the mark of the Antichrist. They are going to suffer forever.

HARVESTING MEANS DIVINE JUDGEMENT

Revelation 14: 13-20:

> *And I heard a voice from heaven saying unto me, Write, Blessed are the dead which die in the Lord from henceforth: Yea, saith the Spirit, that they may rest from their labours; and their works do follow them. And I looked, and behold a white cloud, and upon the cloud one sat like unto the Son of man, having on his head a golden crown, and in his hand a sharp sickle. And another angel came out of the temple, crying with a loud voice to him that sat on the cloud, Thrust in thy sickle, and reap for the time is come for thee to reap; for the harvest of the earth is ripe. And he that sat on the cloud thrust in his sickle on the earth; and the earth was reaped. And another angel came out of the temple which is in heaven, he also having a sharp sickle. And another angel came out from the altar, which had power over fire; and cried with a loud cry to him that had the sharp sickle, saying, Thrust in thy sharp sickle, and gather the clusters of the vine of the earth; for her grapes are fully ripe. And the angel thrust in his sickle into the earth, and gathered the vine of the earth, and cast it into the great winepress of the wrath of God. And the winepress was trodden without the city, and blood came out of the winepress, even unto the horse bridles, by the space of a thousand and six hundred furlongs.*

During the time of the tribulation, men will seek death but they will not be able to die. Many of the saints who refuse the mark of the Antichrist will also suffer terribly. At a certain stage during the tribulation, God will look down in mercy and allow them to die. Death will be for them a welcome thing.

Even now, anyone who dies in Christ and leaves this world suddenly should not be mourned for. Mourners should weep for themselves because if you really belong to Jesus, and you die, you are going into glory. I believe very firmly that death is just a horse that we will ride to bliss.

There are two harvests mentioned here. Jesus will accomplish one. Bible scholars believe that at this stage Jesus is going to take away, through death, all those who remain faithful to Him. This will be the harvest of the tribulation saints. There are Bible passages confirming this.

Matthew 13:24-30:

> *Another parable put he forth unto them, saying, The kingdom of heaven is likened unto a man which sowed good seed in his field: But while men slept, his enemy came and sowed tares among the wheat, and went his way. But when the blade was sprung up, and brought forth fruit, then appeared the tares also. So the servants of the householder came and said unto him, Sir, didst not thou sow good seed in thy field? from whence then hath it tares? He said unto them, An enemy hath done this. The servants said unto him, Wilt thou then that we go and gather them up? But he said, Nay; lest while ye gather up the tares, ye root up also the wheat with them. Let both grow together until the harvest: and in the time of harvest I will say to the reapers, Gather ye together first the tares, and bind them in bundles to burn them: but gather the wheat into my barn.*

Matthew 13:37-43:

> *He answered and said unto them, He that soweth the good seed is the Son of man; The field is the world; the good seed are the children of the kingdom; but the tares are the children of the wicked one; The enemy*

that sowed them is the Devil; the harvest is the end of the world; and the reapers are the angels. As therefore the tares are gathered and burned in the fire; so shall it be in the end of this world. The Son of man shall send forth his angels, and they shall gather out of his kingdom all things that offend, and them which do iniquity; And shall cast them into a furnace of fire: there shall be wailing and gnashing of teeth. Then shall the righteous shine forth as the sun in the kingdom of their Father. Who hath ears to hear, let him hear.

The second harvest concerns all those who are left behind after the tribulation saints are gone. The angel will gather them and throw them into the winepress of God. Whenever the Bible talks about harvesting, it means divine judgement. Several years ago, to get wine out of grapes, you had to tread on them. This is exactly what God is going to do to those who receive the mark of the Antichrist.

All the armies of the nations of the earth will be gathered against Jerusalem for a big battle. This is recorded in Joel 3:2 and 12:

I will also gather all nations, and will bring them down into the valley of Jehoshaphat, and will plead with them there for my people and for my heritage Israel, whom they have scattered among the nations, and parted my land. Let the heathen be wakened, and come up to the valley of Jehoshaphat for there will I sit to judge all the heathen round about.

Zechariah 14:1-4 talks about the Gentile armies gathering together against Jerusalem:

Behold, the day of the LORD cometh, and thy spoil shall be divided in the midst of thee. For I will gather all nations against Jerusalem to battle; and the city shall be taken, and the houses rifled, and the women ravished; and half of the city shall go forth into captivity, and the residue of the people shall not be cut off from the city. Then shall the LORD go forth, and fight against those nations, as when he fought in the day of battle. And his feet shall stand in that day upon the mount of Olives,

> which is before Jerusalem on the east, and the mount of Olives shall cleave in the midst thereof toward the east and toward the west, and there shall be a very great valley; and half of the mountain shall remove toward the north, and half of it toward the south.

When these armies gather, they will be defeated supernaturally. When they are defeated, their blood will form a river. The river will be two hundred miles long and as deep as up to the bridle of horses. From the North to the South of Israel is exactly two hundred miles long. This river of blood will flow from the North to the South of Israel.

Let us go back to the 144,000 people and learn some lessons from them. Firstly, it is not correct that God has no favourites. The scriptures tell us that when Jesus rose from the dead, He appeared to at least five hundred of the brethren. Out of this five hundred, there were seventy that He sent out in pairs, to go and witness. This means that they were special. Out of the seventy were just twelve disciples who were always with Him. Out of the twelve, were particularly close, Peter, James and John. Even among the three, John was the favourite.

It is true that God is no respecter of persons but this is only part of the story. In every nation, those who fear Him are accepted of Him. On the night before Jesus died, He prayed a very significant prayer recorded in John 17. He said that He was praying for the disciples and not for the whole world. Every human being has a potential in them to become a favourite of God. A sanctified person is one who is set apart for Jesus.

Secondly, when you become a favourite of the Most High, it means that you are now entitled to several heavenly privileges. You will be free from all evil because God will take care of you. Isaiah 49:15 says:

> Can a woman forget her sucking child, that she should not have compassion on the son of her womb? yea, they may forget, yet will I not forget thee.

In Isaiah 46:4, the Bible says:

> *And even to your old age I am he; and even to hoar hairs will carry you: I have made, and I will bear; even I will carry, and will deliver you.*

Anybody who tries to harm you is trying to harm God. The Bible says in Isaiah 63:9 that each time the children of God suffer, God also suffers:

> *In all their affliction he was afflicted, and the angel of his presence saved them: in his love and in his pity he redeemed them; and he bare them, and carried them all the days of old.*

Now you will be able to understand why Jesus told Paul on the way to Damascus that he was persecuting Him and not the Christians. When you become the favourite of the Most High, you can relax. With the seal of God on your head, no trouble will be allowed to come near you. 1 Thessalonians 1:10 says:

> *And to wait for his Son from heaven, whom he raised from the dead, even Jesus, which delivered us from the wrath to come.*

Jesus has delivered all His favourites from the wrath to come. We have already been delivered so therefore we shall not go through the tribulation.

Being a favourite of the Most High brings with it a lot of responsibilities on our part. There will never be privileges without responsibilities. Such responsibilities include not being your own again because the owner owns everything that belongs to the favourite. Your time will no longer be yours. Luke 19:13 says:

> *And he called his ten servants, and delivered them ten pounds, and said unto them, Occupy till I come.*

Your money will no longer be your own. Romans 14:12:

> *So then every one of us shall give account of himself to God.*

The words that you speak will no longer be yours. Matthew 12:36:

But I say unto you, That every idle word that men shall speak, they shall give account thereof in the day of judgment.

What exactly does the Bible mean by saying these 144,000 people were virgins? A virgin is a woman who has never known a man or a man who has never known a woman. It is a picture of purity, so we can say that a virgin here is someone who has never backslidden since becoming a Christian. Jesus is willing to restore backsliders but there are two major things to note from the story of the prodigal son. Firstly, he strayed only once and not twice. Secondly, in Luke 15:31, when the elder son was angry, their father said:

And he said unto him, Son thou art ever with me, and all that I have is thine.

This means that nothing belonged to the prodigal son. He came back home as a son without inheritance. Anyone who backslides, after finding out the truth, will lose all their inheritance.

Chapter 27

THE SONG OF MOSES AND THE LAMB

Revelation 15:1-8:

And I saw another sign in heaven, great and marvellous, seven angels having the seven last plagues for in them is filled up the wrath of God. And I saw as it were a sea of glass mingled with fire: and them that had gotten the victory over the beast, and over his image, and over his mark, and over the number of his name, stand on the sea of glass, having the harps of God. And they sing the song of Moses the servant of God, and the song of the Lamb, saying, Great and marvellous are thy works, Lord God Almighty; just and true are thy ways, thou King of saints. Who shall not fear thee, O Lord, and glorify thy name? For thou only art holy: for all nations shall come and worship before thee; for thy judgments are made manifest. And after that I looked, and, behold, the temple of the tabernacle of the testimony in heaven was opened: And the seven angels came out of the temple, having the seven plagues, clothed in pure and white linen, and having their breasts girded with golden girdles. And one of the four beasts gave unto the seven angels seven golden vials full of the wrath of God, who liveth forever and ever. And the temple was filled with smoke from the glory of God, and from his power; and no man was able to enter into the temple, till the seven plagues of the seven angels were fulfilled.

This is the chapter of songs in the Book of Revelation. After the harvesting and the removal of the tribulation saints, they were allowed to join with the saints that had already gone into glory. It was time to rejoice in Heaven. It was time to sing and to praise God. They sang two particular anthems. Moses performed one. Moses will replace Satan in Heaven as the choirmaster of God. Jesus Christ composed the other anthem.

When these people were finishing their praises to God, John saw the Temple in Heaven open and he saw seven angels. One of the four living beings gave the angels seven containers. Inside each container were terrible horrors. The temple in Heaven was filled with smoke. The smoke came from the glory and power of God and it was so intense that no one could go in, until the seven angels finished their assignments. This means that nobody went in to petition God.

The fact that the tribulation saints had been removed before the emergence of the final horrors goes further to confirm that those of us who are ready to depart at the second coming of Jesus will be gone before the problem starts. We have a similar situation in Genesis 7:12-16, during the time of Noah. A single drop of rain did not fall until Noah and his household were safely in the ark. In fact, the Bible says that it was God who shut the door. Likewise, in Genesis 19:15-22 we have the account of Lot. The angels told Lot that the cities of Sodom and Gomorrah would not be destroyed until he had fled.

We are introduced to a sea of glass mingled with fire. We met this sea of glass in Revelation 4:6. There, it was as clear as crystal. Here, it was mingled with fire. Why is this so? This is because God was now in the midst of all the saints. Hebrews 12:29 tells us that our God is a Consuming Fire.

The saints were ready to sing. The first group of people who sang were those who had just passed through the tribulation. They were the victors. Their song was called the song of Moses. This was the song that Moses composed after the children of Israel passed through the Red Sea. This is found in Exodus 15:1-19. Some of our popular hymns and choruses are derived from these verses, including the following:

> I will sing unto the Lord
> For he has triumphed gloriously
> The horse and his rider
> Hath he thrown into the sea.
>
> The God of Abraham, Isaac and Jacob
> Jehovah, the Man of war
> His mercies endureth for ever and ever
> O, Praise the Lord of Hosts
> Alleluia
>
> Who is like unto thee, O Lord?
> Who is like unto thee?
> Among the gods, who is like thee?
> Glorious in holiness
> And fearful in praises
> Doing wonders, Alleluia
>
> Jesus shall reign forever more
> He shall reign forever more.

We will sing many songs in heaven. They will include, "O Lord my God, when I in awesome wonder." We will be saying that He is the King of saints and Lord Almighty.

They said that God's works are great and marvellous. There are several passages in the Bible that tells us about the works of God. For example, Psalm 92:5 says:

> LORD, how great are thy works! and thy thoughts are very deep.

Psalm 98:1:

> O sing unto the LORD a new song; for he hath done marvellous things: his right hand, and his holy arm, hath gotten him the victory.

Psalm 112:2:

> His seed shall be mighty upon earth; the generation of the upright shall be blessed.

Psalm 139:14:

> I will praise thee; for I am fearfully and wonderfully made: marvellous are thy works; and that my soul knoweth right well.

Those of us who have been involved in the ministry and have seen the Almighty God at work on several occasions can never cease to marvel at the power of God to perform miracles, signs and wonders. The ways of God are beyond human comprehension.

The saints went on to ask, "Who shall not fear thee, O Lord and glorify thy name?" The Bible tells us that all nations shall bow down and glorify Him (Psalm 86:9). Our God is supreme the creator of all things. One day, those who oppose God will come face to face with their Maker. He is the One who controls the destiny of the nations. All will bow at the Name of Jesus Christ.

The saints went on to say, "For thou only art holy". The Bible is full of passages about the holiness of God for example, 1 Samuel 2:2 says:

> There is none holy as the LORD: for there is none beside thee: neither is there any rock like our God.

Such sentiments are typical. Our God is a holy God. This is one trait that the Devil cannot imitate. All born again Christians should also be holy.

The saints went on to say that all nations shall come and worship before God. The Bible says in Philippians 2:10-11:

That at the name of Jesus every knee should bow, of things in heaven, and things in earth, and things under the earth; And that every tongue should confess that Jesus Christ is Lord, to the glory of God the Father.

There are many songs based on these verses. One of them is:

> Jesus Christ is Lord
> Jesus Christ is Lord
> Jesus Christ is Lord, Amen
> Every knee should bow
> Every tongue confess
> That Jesus Christ is Lord,
> Alleluia.

THE GLORY OF GOD

As the saints continued to sing, the tabernacle in Heaven was revealed, and suddenly. The glory of God came down. The Bible says that the glory was so awesome that no one could enter the tabernacle until the whole drama on earth was completed (Revelation 15:8). The glory of God is so mighty as to be beyond what any man can comprehend. It is mightier than the midday sun. When it comes down, you dare not remain on your feet.

The glory of God is very difficult to describe. We get a glimpse of what it is like in the account of Saul of Tarsus on the way to Damascus. According to the testimony of Paul, the glory of God was manifested and it was so bright that it reduced the midday sun into darkness. Paul was blinded for three days after the experience.

One day, we are going to be as glorious as the glory of God. 1 John 3:2-3 says:

Beloved, now are we the sons of God, and It doth not yet appear what we shall be: but we know that, when he shall appear, we shall be like him; for we shall see him as he is. And every man that hath this hope in him purifieth himself, even as he is pure.

This is the greatest blessing awaiting all born again Christians. It is no surprise that the saints in Heaven were singing. Those who go to Hell will sing also. They will sing a different song. In pain, they will sing the song of Hell. Not everyone who has heard about the glory of God and the joy of salvation will end up in Heaven. Some will profess faith but backslide. Anyone who lays hands on the plough and looks back is not fit for the Kingdom of God. In other words, there is the appearance of salvation and there is true salvation. Everyday, we must guard against backsliding.

On the last day, there will be a group of people who will be singing forever before the glory of God. I am convinced that by the special grace of God, I will be among them. I pray that you will be also.

Chapter 28

THE WRATH OF GOD

Revelation 16:1-9:

And I heard a great voice out of the temple saying to the seven angels, Go your ways, and pour out the vials of the wrath of God upon the earth. And the first went, and poured out his vial upon the earth; and there fell a noisome and grievous sore upon the men which had the mark of the beast; and upon them which worshipped his image. And the second angel poured out his vial upon the sea; and it became as the blood of a dead man; and every living soul died in the sea. And the third angel poured out his vial upon the rivers and fountains of waters; and they became blood. And I heard the angel of the waters say, Thou art righteous, O Lord, which art, and wast, and shalt be, because thou hast judged thus. For they have shed the blood of saints and prophets, and thou hast given them blood to drink; for they are worthy. And I heard another out of the altar say, Even so, Lord God Almighty, true and righteous are thy judgments. And the fourth angel poured out his vial upon the sun; and power was given unto him to scorch men with fire.

And men were scorched with great heat, and blasphemed the name of God, which hath power over these plagues: and they repented not to give him glory.

There were seven angels holding seven vials filled with the final wrath of God. God allowed these seven angels to pour out this wrath from their vials upon the earth. The people who will go through the last stage of the horrors of the tribulation are those who receive the mark of the Antichrist.

When the first angel poured out the contents of his vial noisome and grievous sores broke out upon those with the mark of the beast. These sores will be so unpleasant that people will cry because of the pain. Some believe that these sores will be caused by radioactive activity as a result of nuclear bombing after the believers have been taken to Heaven.

In 1945 when Hiroshima and Nagasaki were bombed, several thousands of people died. Those who did not die developed certain sores all over their bodies. The sores were incurable and so painful that it was said that those who died were the blessed ones. The bombs that fell on Hiroshima and Nagasaki were much less powerful than the bombs mentioned here. Those who receive the mark of the Antichrist will be around to witness the bombings and sores that will follow.

While they were still crying because of the sores, according to our Bible passage, the second angel poured out the contents of his vial on the earth. Immediately all the seas turned to blood and all living things died. While the people were still filled with surprise, the third angel poured out the contents of his own vial over all rivers and over the source of all waters and they became blood too.

The people on earth at this time will be faced with two major problems. One will be the sores on their bodies and the other will be the lack of water to drink. Because these were people who had shed the blood of many Christians, God will give them blood to drink. The punishment will fit the crime.

While these people were still reeling from this judgement, the fourth angel poured out the contents of his vial on the earth and the heat of the sun increased greatly. With sores on their bodies and no water to drink, the scorching heat would have been intolerable, especially as sores become more painful in extreme heat. Malachi 4:1-2 says, something about this particular time:

> For, behold, the day cometh, that shall burn as an oven; and all the proud, yea, and all that do wickedly, shall be stubble: and the day that cometh shall burn them up, saith the LORD of hosts, that it shall leave them neither root nor branch. But unto you that fear my name shall the Sun of righteousness arise with healing in his wings; and ye shall go forth, and grow up as calves of the stall.

A day is coming when the sun will burn like an oven will burn the wicked ones. This day will come just before the final return of Jesus Christ. It is going to be a very terrible time. Blessed are those who do not live to see this day.

Some people say this cannot happen because God has made provisions to make sure that the amount of heat that comes from the sun to the earth is regulated. Nonetheless, we know that recently scientists have expressed great concern about the destruction of the ozone layer. The ozone layer is what God has put in place round the earth to regulate the heat from the sun. Human beings have damaged this layer through the use of Chlorofluoro Carbons. Steadily, we are working towards what Almighty God has already prescribed.

THE DAY OF GREAT PAIN

Revelation 16:10-21:

> And the fifth angel poured out his vial upon the seat of the beast; and his kingdom was full of darkness; and they gnawed their tongues for pain. And blasphemed the God of heaven because of their pain and

> their sores, and repented not of their deeds. And the sixth angel poured out his vial upon the great river Euphrates; and the water thereof was dried up, that the way of the kings of the east might be prepared. And I saw three unclean spirits like frogs come out of the mouth of the dragon, and out of the mouth of the beast, and out of the mouth of the false prophet. For they are the spirits of Devils, working miracles, which go forth unto the kings of the earth and of the whole world, to gather them to the battle of that great day of God Almighty. Behold, I come as a thief. Blessed is he that watcheth and keepeth his garments, lest he walk naked, and they see his shame. And he gathered them together into a place called in the Hebrew tongue Armageddon. And the seventh angel poured out his vial into the air; and there came a great voice out of the temple of heaven, from the throne, saying, It is done. And there were voices, and thunders, and lightnings; and there was a great earthquake, such as was not since men were upon the earth, so mighty an earthquake, and so great. And the great city was divided into three parts, and the cities of the nations fell: and great Babylon came in remembrance before God, to give unto her the cup of the wine of the fierceness of his wrath. And every island fled away, and the mountains were not found. And there fell upon men a great hail out of heaven, every stone about the weight of a talent: and men blasphemed God because of the plague of the hail; for the plague thereof was exceeding great.

As the people were still battling with pain from their sores, thirst and the heat, a great darkness descended as the vial of the fifth angel was poured out. It was the kind of darkness that you could touch. This did not bring relief because it was another kind of suffering that filled them with terror. The pain of the body is easier to bear than the pain of the mind. This darkness will cover the entire world. In Joel 2.1-2, the Bible says.

> Blow ye the trumpet in Zion, and sound an alarm in my holy mountain: let all the inhabitants of the land tremble: for the day of the LORD

cometh, for it is nigh at hand; A day of darkness and of gloominess, a day of clouds and of thick darkness, as the morning spread upon the mountains: a great people and a strong; there hath not been ever the like, neither shall be any more after it, even to the years of many generations.

Jesus also referred to this day in Mark 13:24:

But in those days, after that tribulation, the sun shall be darkened, and the moon shall not give her light.

Why did God send the sudden darkness? This was for three major reasons, First, the pain from the heat of the sun was so horrible that if it continued too long, the people would die. Since they had not repented, God decided to bring darkness. Second, when the terror of the darkness gripped them and they began to bite their tongues because of the pain, instead of repenting they called God a wicked person. Third, it was to prepare the way for the next judgement.

The sixth angel poured out the contents in his vial and the River Euphrates dried up. The soldiers that will come from the East, that we had earlier mentioned in Revelation 9:16, all two hundred thousand of them, will find the river dried up. This will enable them to cross over for the battle of Armageddon.

In Revelation 16:13-16 an interval is described, which occurs between the action of the sixth angel and that of the seventh. Three unclean spirits came out of the mouth of the unholy trinity. These demons were sent on two major assignments. Firstly, they were to perform miracles Secondly, they were to persuade the kings of the world to come and join in the battle of Armageddon just like the lying spirits in the time of Ahab in 1 Kings 22:20-38.

Be informed that not all miracles are from God. Demons can also perform miracles. The Devil can perform miracles of healing. He can also make you ill, or while you are visiting herbalists, one illness is healed but another substituted. People who claim to be men of God should not be judged by the miracles performed through them but by their lifestyle.

Joel also prophesied concerning this day of great pain in Joel 3:12 and 14-15:

> *Let the heathen he wakened, and come up to the valley of Jehoshaphat: for there will I sit to judge all the heathen round about. Multitudes, multitudes in the valley of decision: for the day of the LORD is near in the valley of decision. The sun and the moon shall he darkened, and the stars shall withdraw their shining.*

When the seventh angel poured out the contents of his vial, there was much hail and an earthquake. A voice then said, "it is done", This statement is different from "it is finished" which Jesus said on the cross. When Jesus said that it was finished, He meant that the work of salvation was completed, "it is done" as said here means that God's wrath against these evil men was fully poured out in judgement.

Certain things then begin to happen. There is a great earthquake, just as Joel said it would be, in Joel 3:16:

> *The LORD also shall roar out of Zion, and utter his voice from Jerusalem; and the heavens and the earth shall shake: but the LORD will be the hope of his people, and the strength of the children of Israel.*

Also, Zechariah 14:4-5:

> *And his feet shall stand in that day upon the mount of Olives, which is before Jerusalem on the east, and the mount of Olives shall cleave in the midst thereof toward the east and toward the west, and there shall be a very great valley; and half of the mountain shall remove toward the north, and half of it toward the south. And ye shall flee to the valley of the mountains; for the valley of the mountains shall reach unto Azal: yea, ye shall flee, like as ye fled from before the earthquake in the days*

of Uzziah king of Judah and the LORD my God shall come, and all the saints with thee.

This earthquake will be the greatest ever to have occurred and it will change the map of the world. Many cities will be destroyed. As a matter of fact, some bible scholars who have studied Ezekiel 47:1-12, believe that cities that will be destroyed include London, Paris, Constantinople and Naples will be among the cities destroyed at this time.

God then starts to fight these evil people from Heaven. Hailstones weighing one hundred pounds are dropped on them. The earth begins to quake. Several nations will be flattened. God has used this method before to fight His battles. An example is in Joshua 10:11 when God used hailstones to fight for Joshua.

Why will God use hailstones against the army that will gather at Armageddon? This is because of what is written in Leviticus 24:16. There is a particular judgement that God has for those who blaspheme His Name:

And he that blasphemeth the name of the LORD, he shall surely be put to death, and all the congregation shall certainly stone him: as well the stranger, as he that is born in the land, when he blasphemeth the name of the LORD, shall be put to death.

Those who blaspheme God are supposed to be put to death by stoning. At this particular time, everyone alive on earth will be blasphemers, and as there will be no one on earth to cast the stones so God will do it Himself.

The most amazing thing is that despite all the deaths and suffering, the few who survive gang up and still call God wicked. They refuse to repent. This means that some people enjoy suffering. Some of us know the will of God yet we do the opposite. When the suffering comes, instead of telling God that we are sorry, we start questioning Him about what we did to deserve being punished.

The Roman Catholic teaching about Purgatory is definitely repudiated here.

This doctrine teaches that if you are not qualified for Heaven, you will go to a place, which is neither Hell nor Heaven where you will suffer for some time. Rome says that as you begin to suffer in this place, you will begin to repent and God will eventually transfer you from purgatory into Heaven. It is clear from our study here that no matter how much some people suffer, they do not repent. We have also seen clearly that there are some people who seem to have a special affinity for suffering. Some people prefer to be forced to do certain things.

We have a few salient lessons to learn from Revelation 16. For example, one could begin to wonder why God, whose name is Love, would unleash this kind of judgement on human beings who are His creation. The first thing that we have to note about God's judgement is that it demonstrates His love. The Bible tells us that whoever the father loves, He chastises (Hebrews 12:6). If you love your son and he does wrong, it is your duty to correct him as an act of love. Many a time, good correction will involve pain, particularly for the one who is being corrected. At times, the one making the correction will also feel pain too. God does not want sinners to perish.

The second thing we have to note about the judgement of God is that His goal is the restoration of the sinner. God has no pleasure in the death of a sinner but that such a sinner should repent and live. God knows that as long as you remain in sin, He cannot bless you. If he does not show you that you are wrong by punishing you, you may think you are actually doing the right thing. As a matter of fact, if you are committing sin and there is no punishment following immediately, you need to check whether you are still a child of God or not. It could mean that God has already withdrawn from you.

In Revelation 16, the Bible repeatedly says that the people did not repent. This means that what God was expecting from them was repentance. This shows that, thirdly, God punishes the sinner so as to prevent greater horrors from happening to him or her in future. For example, God brought the punishment thick and fast on the people so that they would repent and avoid eternity in Hell. All they were going through was just a preparation for the real suffering. God was showing them that there is pain and thirst in Hell, He did this to give them a chance to repent.

Someone once said that it was love that compelled God to drive Adam and Eve out of the Garden of Eden. This is because, if they had eaten out of the fruit of life, they would have lived for ever in their fallen state. For many people today, death is a welcome escape from suffering.

Moreover, God punishes sinners in order to turn them from their sin, which is the sting of death. If you sin, God punishes you and you make up your mind not to sin again, the sting has been taken out of death for you. Whatever time death may come you have nothing to fear because you know that you are going into glory.

Furthermore, when God punishes a sinner and the sinner repents and begins to live a holy life, the way is opened for the anointing of God to flow to such a person, Hebrews 1:9 says:

> *Thou hast loved righteousness, and hated iniquity; therefore God, even thy God, hath anointed thee with the oil of gladness above thy fellows.*

If God wants to use you and He wants His anointing to flow in your life, He will not tolerate these little sins. As a matter of fact, if God really loves you, if you sin, punishment comes quickly.

Also, the justice of God shows His faithfulness. How can severe judgement show that God is faithful? Because God had already said that He would always fulfil His promises. What we fail to realise is that the promises of God are two-fold. One of the promises of God is that if you sin you will be punished. Another promise is that if you do well you will prosper. There are several passages in the Bible that juxtaposes both promises. For example, Psalm 34:19 says:

> *Many are the afflictions of the righteous: but the LORD delivereth him out of them all.*

Isaiah 3:11:

Woe unto the wicked! it shall be ill with him: for the reward of his hands shall be given him.

Isaiah 3:10:

Say ye to the righteous, that it shall be well with him for they shall eat the fruit of their doings.

Psalm 34:21:

Evil shall slay the wicked; and they that hate the righteous shall be desolate.

Our God, who is so faithful to fulfil His promises to the wicked, will surely bring to pass His promises to the righteous in our lives. Therefore, the choice is not actually in the hands of God but in our hands. Isaiah 1:18-20 says:

Come now, and let us reason together, saith the LORD: though your sins be as scarlet, they shall be as white as snow; though they be red like crimson, they shall be as wool. If ye be willing and obedient, ye shall eat the good of the land: But if ye refuse and rebel, ye shall be devoured with the sword: for the mouth of the LORD hath spoken it.

You have to choose whether to be obedient to Him and prosper, or to do what pleases you. You should not blame God for whatever is the consequence of your sin. Most of us are in the situation that we are now because we know the will of God and are not doing it.

I believe that most of our problems will be solved if we would only repent and come to Jesus. Our God prefers to bless us than to punish us. He is a God of love.

Chapter 29

THE BABYLONIAN CULT

Revelation 17:1-6:

And there came one of the seven angels which had the seven vials, and talked with me, saying unto me, Come hither; I will show unto thee the judgment of the great whore that sitteth upon many waters: With whom the kings of the earth have committed fornication, and the inhabitants of the earth have been made drunk with the wine of her fornication. So he carried me away in the spirit into the wilderness: and I saw a woman sit upon a scarlet coloured beast, full of names of blasphemy, having seven heads and ten horns. And the woman was arrayed in purple and scarlet colour, and decked with gold and precious stones and pearls, having a golden cup in her hand full of abominations and filthiness of her fornication: And upon her forehead was a name written, MYSTERY, BABYLON THE GREAT, THE MOTHER OF HARLOTS AND ABOMINATIONS OF THE EARTH. And I saw the woman drunken with the blood of the saints, and with the blood of the martyrs of Jesus: and when I saw her, I wondered with great admiration:

The Last Days

In Revelation 17:4. the Bible tells us about a woman dressed in scarlet and purple. Included in the Papal regalia are scarlet garments with many pearls and precious stones. The woman was also said to be drunk with the blood of saints. Anyone who has ever read of the Inquisition would have read that there was a time when the Pope said that anyone who refused to be a Roman Catholic must be killed.

Millions of people were killed. The blood shed by the Church of Rome has been greater than that shed by Hitler. In verse 9, we are told that the city was on seven hills. Those who have been to Rome can observe that the city is built on seven hills.

In summary, what the Bible is saying is that there will be two categories of people at the end of the age. There will be those who are born again, who will be the bride of Jesus. All the others, after the bride has gone will be join together and form one false Church with its headquarters in Rome. This is the woman that will marry the Antichrist.

At the end of Revelation 17 we note that the Antichrist himself will destroy his bride. This is to tell us that the Devil loves no one. If the Devil is using you and you are enjoying it, one day, he will turn round and tear you into pieces. All those who serve the Devil are going to end up in Hell.

Chapter 30

THE FALL OF BABYLON (Revelation 18:1-10)

And after these things I saw another angel come down from heaven, having great power; and the earth was lightened with his glory. And he cried mightily with a strong voice, saying, Babylon the great is fallen, is fallen, and is become the habitation of devils, and the hold of every foul spirit, and a cage of every unclean and hateful bird. For all nations have drunk of the wine of the wrath of her fornication, and the kings of the earth have committed fornication with her, and the merchants of the earth are waxed rich through the abundance of her delicacies. And I heard another voice from heaven, saying, Come out of her, my people, that ye be not partakers of her sins, and that ye receive not of her plagues. For her sins have reached unto heaven, and God hath remembered her iniquities. Reward her even as she rewarded you, and double unto her double according to her works: in the cup which she hath filled fill to her double. How much she hath glorified herself, and lived deliciously, so much torment and sorrow give her: for she saith in her heart, I sit a queen, and am no widow, and shall see no sorrow.

therefore shall her plagues come in one day, death, and mourning, and famine; and she shall be utterly burned with fire: for strong is the Lord God who judgeth her. And the kings of the earth, who have committed fornication and lived deliciously with her, shall bewail her, and lament for her, when they shall see the smoke of her burning, Standing afar off for the fear of her torment, saying, Alas, alas, that great city Babylon, that mighty city! for in one hour is thy judgment come.

Revelation chapter 18 describes the fall of a city. The first thing that we note in this chapter is that there is a religious system called Babylon. Also, there is a particular city called Babylon. What we see here is the use of the same words to describe a city and its dwellers. The Bible makes it clear that it is the Antichrist that will destroy the religious system called Babylon, once he seizes power. It is God who is going to destroy the city called Babylon. Is this Babylon mentioned here going to be rebuilt? The original Babylon has already been destroyed yet God is saying that during the tribulation, Babylon is going to be demolished. Some Bible scholars believe that a new Babylon will be built. With the technlogy available now, it would be easy to do so. There was an article in the Los Angeles Times of December 2 1971 about the rising Tower of Babel. We were informed that the government of Iraq was planning to rebuild part of the ruins of Babylon, including constucting a 295 feet tower.

Also, this school of thought based its premise on Isaiah 13:1 and 6-7

The burden of Babylon, which Isaiah the son of Amoz did see. Howl ye; for the day of the LORD is at hand; it shall come as a destruction from the Almighty. Therefore shall all hands be faint, and every man's heart shall melt.

Some people believe that there must be a rebuilt Babylon in existence before Christ returns. Other scholars believe that there is Babylon on earth already. They say this is Rome, the headquarters of the Roman Catholic Church. If we study the history of Rome to see whether it tallies with what God says in our Bible passage.

The city of Babylon was accused of being too wealthy. Among the items traded included men and the souls of men. There is an old saying that out of ten measures of the riches of the world, nine went to Rome. In other words, if you divide the whole wealth of the world into ten parts, nine parts will be found in Rome.

The richest organisation in the world is the Roman Catholic Church. It is richer than many countries of the world combined. Its wealth is measured in trillions. Another quotation from an historian says that the most extravagant luxury of today is abject poverty compared to the prodigal magnificence of ancient Rome.

The wealth of ancient Rome cannot be compared to the wealth of today. In those days, merchandise was brought from all corners of the world to Rome. In fact, it was said that if there was anything you were looking for and you did not find it in Rome, it meant that the thing did not exist or never existed. There was a time when Nero held a banquet and the cost of the flowers used to decorate the eating area alone was £35,000. At this time, the average expenditure of an emperor was £20 million per annum.

When Nero wanted to fish, he used a golden net. His horses wore shoes made of silver. A banquet of guests in those days was not complete without the serving of the brains of peacocks and the tongues of nightingales. These are very rare and costly birds. In those days, they even dissolved pearls into wine to show that they drank money. Revelation 17:7-17

> *And the angel said unto me, Wherefore didst thou marvel? I will tell thee the mystery of the woman, and of the beast that carrieth her, which hath the seven heads and ten horns. The beast that thou sawest was, and is not; and shall ascend out of the bottomless pit, and go into perdition: and they that dwell on the earth shall wonder, whose names were not written in the book of life from the foundation of the world, when they behold the beast that was, and is not, and yet is. And here is the mind which hath wisdom. The seven heads are seven mountains,*

on which the woman sitteth. And there are seven kings: five are fallen, and one is, and the other is not yet come; and when he cometh, he must continue a short space. And the beast that was, and is not, even he is the eighth, and is of the seven, and goeth into perdition. And the ten horns which thou sawest are ten kings, which have received no kingdom as yet; but receive power as kings one hour with the beast. These have one mind, and shall give their power and strength unto the beast. These shall make war with the Lamb, and the Lamb shall overcome them: for he is Lord of lords, and King of kings: and they that are with him are called, and chosen, and faithful. And he saith unto me, The waters which thou sawest, where the whore sitteth, are peoples, and multitudes, and nations, and tongues. And the ten horns which thou sawest upon the beast, these shall hate the whore, and shall make her desolate and naked, and shall eat her flesh, and burn her with fire. For God hath put in their hearts to fulfil his will, and to agree, and give their kingdom unto the beast, until the words of God shall be fulfilled.

There are many grave things in this chapter. We shall point to some of them now before we look at them in detail.

Some Bible scholars believe that the description we have in verse 8 above is of the Antichrist. They even go on to say that the Antichrist will be none other than a reincarnation of Judas Iscariot. They say that Judas is suffering somewhere and is to be brought out by God to do something that He had already planned.

As for verse 10, some Bible scholars also believe that the seven kings mentioned refer to seven popes. Five of them will be prominent, one will rule for a short time and out of the seventh one will come the eight one. They say the one that will be there for a short time has already come and gone. There was a pope that died three months after he was ordained – some had even shorter reigns: 12 days in one instance.

According to verse 17, whatever the evil ones will be doing during the tribulation is subject to the will of God. In other words, everything happening here on earth is under the absolute control of God and will always be under His absolute control. This is one thing that encourages me. God is in control of my life. Is He in control of your life? If so, it means that nothing can happen to you in this world unless God allows it. This is the proof that only good will happen to those of us who are His own.

We can now go into a detailed study of the chapter. One of the seven angels came to John and said that he wanted to show him certain things. The angels showed him a woman whose name was, MYSTERY, BABYLON THE GREAT, THE MOTHER OF HARLOTS AND ABOMINATIONS OF THE EARTH. There are many mysteries in the Bible. One great mystery is that Jesus is going to have a bride. The Jews and the old prophets never knew about this fact. They thought the Jews were the bride of Jehovah and that there was no hope for the Gentiles. God, however, had a plan to marry His Son to both Jews and Gentiles. This was revealed to Paul in Ephesians 3:3-6:

> *How that by revelation he made known unto me the mystery; (as I wrote afore in few words. Whereby, when ye read, ye may understand my knowledge in the mystery of Christ) Which in other ages was not made known unto the sons of men, as it is now revealed unto his holy apostles and prophets by the Spirit; That the Gentiles should be fellow heirs, and of the same body, and partakers of his promise in Christ by the gospel.*

The Antichrist is also going to have a bride. This was not revealed to Paul but to John. This is why he also called it a mystery. The name of the bride of Christ is called, Holy Jerusalem. Look at Revelation 21:9-10:

> *And there came unto me one of the seven angels which had the seven vials full of the seven last plagues, and talked with me, saying, Come hither, I will shew time the bride, the Lamb's wife. And he carried me away in the spirit to a great and high mountain, and showed me that great city, the holy Jerusalem, descending out of heaven from God.*

The Last Days

The bride of the Antichrist is called, 'Babylon the Great.' This name symbolises all those who do not accept the true gospel of Jesus Christ. There is no way that they can avoid being married to the Antichrist.

Why Babylon? A certain man called Nimrod built Babylon or Babel. This is recorded in Genesis 10:8-10. Nimrod, whose name means, strong or mighty, was a great hunter. He hunted for the soul of men. He married his mother and for this, his uncle killed him. It was Nimrod and his followers who decided to build the Tower of Babel. They decided to settle down in one place, contrary to the plan of God who decreed that man should replenish the earth and cover it.

They recollected that the last time they disobeyed God, He destroyed the earth with water. So, they wanted to build a tower so high that if another flood were to take place, they would not drown. When Nimrod died, his mother said he did not die. This was the beginning of the Babylonian cult. The adherents of this cult claimed to know the wisdom and the secrets of God. To join the cult you had to make a confession of all the evil you had ever done to their priest.

Once you confessed to the priest, he had a hold on you. If you ever dared to say that you wanted to leave the cult, he would reveal all your secrets. This was the origin of the Roman Catholic sacrament of confession, today. The title of the leader of the Babylonian cult was the Pontiff.

The headquarters of Satan was in Babylon. When the Babylonian Empire fell, Satan then transferred his headquarters to Pergamos. The last ruler of Pergamos, Attalos III was also called the Pontiff. He died in BC133 but before he died he transferred the headquarters of the Babylonian cult to Rome. A certain man called Julius Caesar became Pontiff in B.C. 63. He also became the leader of the secret society which is part of the cult. This was how he was able to conquer so many cities. All the Emperors of Rome after Julius Caesar were heads of the Babylonian cult until AD376. when the Emperor Gratian became a Christian.

Gratian could have become the Pontiff but he refused. The Bishop of the church in Rome decided that if the emperor did not want to become Pontiff, he would assume the post. The Bishop was called Damasus. You may wonder how a bishop could become the head of a secret society. This bishop was able to secure his position because he was a member of the cult. He had been appointed bishop by the monks of Mount Carmel, which Jezebel had established. Within three years, all the rituals of the Babylonian cult came into the church. For example, they started the worship of the Virgin Mary in A.D. 381.

On one occasion, someone drank wine with a pearl worth £80,000 dissolved in it. There was another occasion when there were sixty million slaves in the Roman Empire. Human beings were sold like goats. The rich had slaves to do everything, including reading and memorising. Slaves were also used for sacrifices.

All this make scholars believe that Rome is the Babylon that God was referring to in Revelation 18. It does not matter, however, whether it is Rome or a new Babylon that is going to be built. One thing that is certain is that it is going to be destroyed. There have been several prophecies concerning the fall of Babylon:

Isaiah 13:19-22:

> *And Babylon, the glory of kingdoms, the beauty the Chaldees' excellency, shall be as when God overthrew Sodom and Gomorrah. It shall never be inhabited, neither shall it be dwelt in from generation to generation: neither shall the Arabian pitch tent there; neither shall the shepherds make their fold there. But wild beasts of the desert shall lie there; and their houses shall be full of doleful creatures; and owls shall dwell there, and satyrs shall dance there. And the wild beasts of the islands shall cry in their desolate houses, and dragons in their pleasant palaces: and her time is near to come, and her days shall not be prolonged.*

Jeremiah 50:39:

> *Therefore the wild beasts of the desert with the wild beasts of the Islands shall dwell there, and the owls shall dwell therein: and it shall be no more inhabited for ever; neither shall it be dwelt in from generation to generation.*

Jeremiah 51:37:

> *And Babylon shall become heaps, a dwelling place for dragons, an astonishment, and an hissing, without an inhabitant.*

The destruction of Babylon is going to come suddenly. It is going to disappear at a stroke. Nowadays, this kind of destruction is possible. One nuclear bomb can do the job.

There are a lot of lessons to learn from this chapter. Firstly, with reference to verse 4, God always calls on His own before destruction comes. The Almighty God will not begin to destroy until He has given the call to His people to flee. If He invites you to come and you reject the invitation, then God will be justified if He destroys you along with sinners.

The Bible is full of several examples of the Almighty God calling people out before devastation strikes. There is the example of Lot in Genesis 19:12-14. Angels sent by God told Lot that the cities of Sodom and Gomorrah would not be destroyed until he and his family had fled the city.

Secondly, God knows how to separate the righteous from the sinners when He wants to bring in His judgement. If you do not partake in sin, you will not face punishment. The Bible says that even though hand join in hand, the wicked shall not be unpunished (Proverbs 11:21). It shows again that our God is righteous. He will not punish the righteous instead of the sinner.

This is also illustrated in Numbers 16:23-35. These verses describe the rebellion of Korah, Dathan and Abiram against Moses. They accused Moses of putting his relatives into positions of leadership over the Israelites. Many people joined the rebellion. It was only after there was a clear demarcation between those on the side of Moses and those on the side of the rebels that God brought judgement. The ground opened and the rebels were swallowed up. It seems that as the Church Age coming to an end, a spirit of rebellion is being let loose in the world.

Isaiah 48:20 is an important scripture for consideration:

> *Go ye forth of Babylon, flee ye from the Chaldeans, with a voice of singing declare ye, tell this, utter it even to the end of the earth; say ye, The LORD hath redeemed his servant Jacob.*

Here, Almighty God gives a call to all His people that we will need to think very deeply before we decide to stay in an organisation that we know operates contrary to the will of God. If it is abundantly clear to you that you are worshipping in a place where the doctrine and practise is contrary to the will of God, and you stay on, when judgement falls, you may not be spared. You may think that you will change the organisation from within but this is not easy if you are not a leader in the organisation.

The Bible says that we should not be unequally yoked with unbelievers (2 Corinthians 6:14). We are to keep ourselves pure (1 Timothy 5:22). Also, Romans 12:2 says:

> *And be not conformed to this world: but be ye transformed by the renewing of your mind, that ye may prove what is that good, and acceptable, and perfect, will of God.*

Do not conform. If you act according to the way of the world, when the time of judgement comes, you will be punished with the world. Instead, you are to be transformed and renewed. You should learn to reject the ways of the world so you will be safe. Jeremiah 51:44-45 says:

> *And I will punish Bel in Babylon, and I will bring forth out of his mouth that which he hath swallowed up: and the nations shall not flow together any more unto him: yea, the wall of Babylon shall fall. My*

people, go ye out of the midst of her, and deliver ye every man his soul from the fierce anger of the LORD.

God is simply saying here that you should flee from His anger. When the city of Babylon was being destroyed, as recorded in our Bible passage, the people stood afar, mourning. They were mourning because they would not be able to enjoy themselves anymore. All their wealth had vanished in a single day.

Wealth is useless on the day of judgement. The Bible says that we brought nothing into this world and we will depart with nothing (I Timothy 6:7). If you are wise, you should use whatever God has given to you for Him. Money will be useless to you when you die. When you die, friends may mourn and wail but they will not die with you. None of the kings and merchants was ready to die with Babylon.

Those who weep when you die are likely to do so for selfish reasons. Some mourn because the assistance they were getting will no longer be available. They mourn for themselves. These are the friends that prevent many from doing the will of God.

There is only one Friend who will go through the valley of death with you. His Name is Jesus. You should follow Him because on the last day, He is the One who will welcome you to Heaven. None of your friends will be able to help you on the day of judgement.

The men of Babylon mourned because all the things they lusted after had suddenly disappeared (Revelation 18:14). There are lessons to be learnt here also. Those who lust after material things will discover that even after they have obtained what they wanted, they are not satisfied. Also, there are many people who struggle very hard to gain wealth but when they arrive at the stage of considering themselves wealthy, they begin to have all kinds of illness and diseases that make it impossible for them to enjoy their wealth.

There are a few examples of people like this in the Bible. For example Gehazi in 2 Kings 5:25-27. Gehazi lusted after wealth. He could not enjoy the wealth when he got it because he became a leper. Another example is Judas Iscariot. He was paid thirty pieces of silver but never spent any of them (Matthew 27:3-8). The Bible says clearly that we should not love the world or things of the world because they will prevent us from loving God (1 John 2:15-17). The things of the world will pass away but the Almighty God will be there forever more. Jeremiah 17:11 says:

> *As the partridge sitteth on eggs, and hatcheth them not; so he that getteth riches, and not by right, shall leave them in the midst of his days, and at his end shall be a fool.*

Those who gain wealth through illegitimate means will die in the middle of their years, they will become fools. We should pray that God does not give us the wealth that will draw us away from Him.

Chapter 31

THE MARRIAGE OF THE LAMB

Revelation 19:1-10:

> *And after these things I heard a great voice of much people in heaven, saying, Alleluia; Salvation, and glory, and honour, and power, unto the Lord our God: For true and righteous are his judgments: for he hath judged the great whore, which did corrupt the earth with her fornication, and hath avenged the blood of his servants at her hand. And again they said, Alleluia. And her smoke rose up for ever and ever. And the four and twenty elders and the four beasts fell down and worshipped God that sat on the throne, saying, Amen; Alleluia. And a voice came out of the throne, saying, Praise our God, all ye his servants, and ye that fear him, both small and great. And I heard as it were the voice of a great multitude, and as the voice of many waters, and as the voice of mighty thunderings, saying, Alleluia: for the Lord God omnipotent reigneth. Let us be glad and rejoice, and give honour to him: for the marriage of the Lamb is come, and his wife hath made herself ready. And to her was granted that she should be arrayed in fine*

linen, clean and white: for the fine linen is the righteousness of saints. And he saith unto me, Write, Blessed are they which are called unto the marriage supper of the Lamb. And he saith unto me. These are the true sayings of God. And I fell at his feet to worship him. And he said unto me. See thou do it not: I am thy fellowservant, and of thy brethren that have the testimony of Jesus: worship God: for the testimony of Jesus is the spirit of prophecy.

After the destruction of Babylon the Great, the Mother of Harlots and headquarters of the Antichrist, there was an invitation to those in Heaven. They were told to rejoice because God has avenged them (Revelation 18:20). When the invitation came, they responded with the shout of 'Halleluia'. The word, halleluia, is made up of two sections; 'Hallelu' is the second person imperative masculine plural form of the Hebrew verb 'Hallel', meaning praise and 'jah' which means Jehovah. Thus we have the phrase, 'Praise Jehovah'.

In the original Bible, 'alleluia' is written in twenty-four places in the Old Testament and in only four places in the New Testament, all in the Book of Revelation. In the Old Testament it is written as, 'Praise ye the Lord'. (Psalm 106:1, Psalm 112.1, Psalm 113:1, Psalm l46:1, Psalm 147:1. Psalm 148:1, Psalm 149:1 and 9, Psalm 150:1).

The first 'alleluia' in Revelation 19 was sung at the destruction of the bride of Antichrist, Babylon the Great, Mother of Harlots. She was judged because she corrupted the world. The second and third halleluias were sung when the city of Babylon was destroyed. This fulfilled the prophecy in Isaiah 34:9-10:

And the streams thereof shall be turned into pitch, and the dust thereof into brimstone, and the land thereof shall become burning pitch. It shall not be quenched night nor day; the smoke thereof shall go up for ever: from generation to generation it shall lie waste; none shall pass through it for ever and ever.

The Last Days

The third 'alleluia' sounded like a thunderclap and the roar of many waters. It was sung to celebrate that the Lord God Omnipotent reigns. The shout was very loud because of the forthcoming marriage of the Lamb. It was also loud because the bride had made herself ready. There will be no disappointments for the bride because the Bridegroom is also ready.

The voice from the throne that said, 'Praise our God' called on three groups of people. He called on all His servants. These are the prophets (Revelation 10:7, Revelation 11:18, Revelation 22:6) and martyrs (Revelation 7:3, Revelation 19:2). The voice also called on all who fear Him both small and great. This refers to Christians of all stages in life. This means that as long as we are believers, no matter which category we fall into, we must shout, Halleluia. The response to the call in Heaven is described by John as sounding like the voice of a great multitude. It also like the voice of many waters and thunder.

Why should you shout before this takes place? This is because the day of the marriage of the Lamb can come at any time. It may be today. Even if it is not today, with every day that passes, we move a step closer to Heaven, while those that are not born again move a step closer to Hell. In the past, the prophet God depicted a picture of God marrying Man. Hosea 2:19-20:

> *And I will betroth thee unto me for ever; yea, I will betroth thee unto me in righteousness, and in judgment, and in lovingkindness, and in mercies. I will even betroth thee unto me in faithfulness: and thou shall know the LORD.*

God has been talking about this marriage for a long time. In Isaiah 54:5 is written:

> *For thy Maker is thine husband; the LORD of hosts is his name; and thy Redeemer the Holy One of Israel; The God of the whole earth shall he be called.*

Jesus Christ talked about the wedding. In Matthew 22 He told a parable about a marriage feast. He also talked of the wedding garment. In Mark 2:18-19 the Bible says:

> *And the disciples of John and of the Pharisees used to fast: and they come and say unto him, Why do the disciples of John and of the Pharisees fast, but thy disciples fast not? And Jesus said unto them, Can the children of the bridechamber fast, while the Bridegroom is with them? as long as they have the Bridegroom with them, they cannot fast.*

In Matthew 25:1 we have the story of the ten virgins and the Bridegroom:

> *Then shall the kingdom of heaven be likened unto ten virgins, which took their lamps, and went forth to meet the Bridegroom.*

John 3:27-29 talks about the friends of the Bridegroom:

> *John answered and said, A man can receive nothing, except it be given him from heaven. Ye yourselves bear me witness, that I said, I am not the Christ, but that I am sent before him. He that hath the bride is the bridegroom: but the friend of the bridegroom, which standeth and heareth him, rejoiceth greatly because of the bridegroom's voice: this my joy therefore is fulfilled.*

In 2 Corinthians 11:2, the Holy Spirit took up the same theme. Paul called the Church a pure virgin for Christ:

> *For I am jealous over you with godly jealousy: for I have espoused you to one husband, that I may present you as a chaste virgin to Christ.*

In Ephesians 5:23-32. the marriage of Christ and the Church is presented to us as the model marriage.

There are several things to note about this wedding. First and foremost, it is the marriage of the Lamb and not that of the bride. Most of the time, when people talk about a wedding, the emphasis is on the woman who is getting married. The plan of God from ages past is that His Son will get married (Ephesians 1:3-4).

Secondly, it is because of this wedding that Jesus became a man. You may say He came to redeem sinners and to destroy the work of the Devil, but He did these things so as to marry us. He went back to Heaven as a man, and remains a man. 1 Timothy 2:5 says:

For there is one God, and one mediator between God and men, the man Christ Jesus.

Furthermore, the courtship between Jesus and His bride is the longest that the world has ever known. He has been waiting for almost two thousand years already, even though He has paid the bride price. In the story of the ten virgins, we are told that the Bridegroom tarried (Matthew 25:1-5). He is tarrying so as to increase the number of those who will make up the bride.

Also, the bride price is the costliest ever known. He gave His total life savings as a bride price. He made available to His bride all the heritage of His Father. We are joint heirs with Him (Romans 8:16-17, 1 Corinthians 6:20). He also paid with His life. 1 Peter 1:18-19 says:

Forasmuch as ye know that ye were not redeemed with corruptible things, as silver and gold, from your vain conversation received by tradition from your fathers; But with the precious blood of Christ, as of a lamb without blemish and without spot.

If you are willing to pay a price for a bride, the bride must be really beautiful and precious. I am very handsome, precious and important to Jesus. If I were otherwise. Jesus would not pay such a bride price for me.

Moreover, this wedding is going to be the greatest royal wedding ever. This is because it is the Son of the King of kings and the heir to the throne of the universe that is getting married to princes and princesses. It is also the wedding that will join the Kingdom of Heaven to the kingdom of the world.

In every wedding, there is someone to give the bride away. Our original father was the Devil and he cannot come to this wedding. The Bible tells us that all that were born of women are unclean and conceived in sin (Psalm 51:5). This is why we use the term 'born again' to describe the process of becoming a Christian.

Nevertheless, Jesus will tell God the Father that He is the one getting married to us on His own. Ephesians 5:25-27 confirms this:

> *Husbands, love your wives, even as Christ also loved the church, and gave himself for it; That he might sanctify and cleanse it with the washing of water by the word, That he might present it to himself a glorious church, not having spot, or wrinkle, or any such thing; but that it should be holy and without blemish.*

Finally, the bride will make herself ready. It is not the Bridegroom that will make the bride ready. It is the responsibility of the bride to make herself ready. It will be too sad if Jesus comes and you are not ready. The bride must make herself ready or there will be no wedding for her. In the parable of the ten virgins, when the Bridegroom came, the five virgins that were ready went with him and the door was then shut. When the other five finally made themselves ready, it was too late; the door was not opened for them.

The bride that Jesus is returning for must be spotlessly clean and holy (Ephesians 5:27). 1 Peter 1:13-16 says:

> *Wherefore gird up the loins of your mind, be sober, and hope to the end for the grace that is to be brought unto you at the revelation of Jesus Christ; As obedient children, not fashioning yourselves according to the former lusts in your ignorance: But as he which hath called you is holy, so be ye holy in all manner of conversation; Because it is written, Be ye holy; for I am holy.*

Moreover, the bride must be obediently doing the will of God till the Bridegroom comes. Ephesians 2:12-15:

> *That at that time ye were without Christ, being aliens from the*

commonwealth of Israel, and strangers from the covenants of promise, having no hope, and without God in the world: But now in Christ Jesus ye who sometimes were far off are made nigh by the blood of Christ. For he is our peace, who hath made both one, and hath broken down the middle wall of partition between us; Having abolished in his flesh the enmity, even the law of commandments contained in ordinances; for to make in himself of twain one new man, so making peace;

Chapter 32

CHRISTIANS ARE WINNERS

Revelation 19:7-14:

Let us be glad and rejoice, and give honour to him: for the marriage of the Lamb is come, and his wife hath made herself ready. And to her was granted that she should be arrayed in fine linen, clean and white: for the fine linen is the righteousness of saints. And he saith unto me, Write, Blessed are they which are called unto the marriage supper of the Lamb. And he saith unto me, These are the true sayings of God. And I fell at his feet to worship him. And I fell at his feet to worship him. And he said unto me, See thou do it not: I am thy fellowservant, and of thy brethren that have the testimony of Jesus: worship God: for the testimony of Jesus is the spirit of prophecy. And I saw heaven opened, and behold a white horse; and he that sat upon him was called Faithful and True, and in righteousness he doth judge and make war. His eyes were as a flame of fire, and on his head were many crowns; and he had a name written, that no man knew, but he himself. And he was clothed with a vesture dipped in blood: and his name is called The Word of God.

In verse 8 above, we are told that the bride was robed in clean white linen and that this fine linen is the righteousness of saints. What do we learn from this? Many of us know already that each person we win for Christ is going to be a jewel in our crown when we get to Heaven. Some crowns will be so full of stars that it will be difficult to look at them. Some crowns will be without stars because the owners never saw anyone come to faith.

What of the dress that we will wear? The quality of the dress that we will wear will be determined by the other works that we do here, in our Christian life, apart from soul winning. All our good works after we came to faith are recorded by God. The evil that we did before becoming a Christian are remembered no more.

In fact, when we get to Heaven, we will wear two types of dresses. Everyone will have the one we call underwear, which is like a shirt under a jacket, but our good works will determine the quality of the second dress, which is like the jacket. Galatians 6:6-10:

> *Let him that is taught in the word communicate unto him that teacheth in all good things. Be not deceived; God is not mocked: for whatsoever a man soweth, that shall he also reap. For he that soweth to his flesh shall of the flesh reap corruption; but he that soweth to the Spirit shall of the Spirit reap life everlasting. And let us not be weary in well doing: for in due season we shall reap, if we faint not. As we have therefore opportunity, let us do good unto all men, especially unto them who are of the household of faith.*

I pray that your reward will be a glorious one, in Jesus' Name.

In verse 10 of Revelation 19, John said he fell down when he saw the beauty of the marriage of the Lamb. He fell down at the feet of an angel that was showing him these things. The angel told him not to worship him because he was just an angel. You are only to worship God. There are many people who worship angels. This is a ridiculous thing to do. Hebrews 1:13-14 tells us that angels are the servants of those of us who are to inherit the

Kingdom of God. No matter what they do for us, we must not worship them.

The angel also said that the testimony of Jesus is the spirit of prophecy. This is a guide as to whether a prophecy is true or false. Many Christians do not know when a prophecy is correct or not. Every prophecy must agree with the testimony of Jesus. It must be in line with the teaching of the Bible. In 1 Corinthians 14:3, we read:

> *But he that prophesieth speaketh unto men to edification, and exhortation, and comfort.*

A true prophecy must edify, exhort and comfort. All prophecies point to Jesus. All prophecies should start with Jesus and end with Him.

John said he saw Heaven open and saw someone on a white horse. A white horse speaks of a victorious captain. Some have asked whether Jesus will ride on a white horse when coming back. Are there horses in Heaven? Yes, there are horses in Heaven, and Jesus will come back again riding on a white horse. 2 Kings 2:11 says:

> *And it came to pass, as they still went on, and talked, that, behold, there appeared a chariot of fire, and horses of fire, and parted them both asunder; and Elijah went up by a whirlwind into heaven.*

In 2 Kings 6, when a king ordered the arrest of Elisha and his servant saw a whole army surround them, God did something, as recorded in 2 Kings 6:17:

> *And Elisha prayed, and said, LORD, I pray thee, open his eyes, that he may see. And the LORD opened the eyes of the young man; and he saw: and, behold, the mountain was full of horses and chariots of fire round about Elisha.*

These horses came from Heaven.

Jesus will come back on a horse during the second stage of His second coming. Revelation 19:14 tells us that the hosts of Heaven will follow Him on white horses too. I will be one of them. Our Captain, Lord and Master, will be riding in front on His own white horse while we will be following.

After the marriage, we will go on honeymoon. God has decided in His own infinite wisdom that the honeymoon will take place here on earth. We will all come back to earth in our robes and our white horses. The honeymoon will last for a thousand years.

Earlier on it was noted that Jesus will ride a white horse to show that He is the Victor and the real Overcomer. He deserves to call Himself by the title because He told us in John 16:33 that He has overcome the world. He also said in Revelation 1:18 that He has overcome death and the Devil. The one who has overcome the world, death and the Devil definitely is the true Overcomer.

Why will we also be riding white horses? We will be on white horses because we are also overcomers. Romans 8:37 says we are more than conquerors. We are more than conquerors because the real Conqueror is our Husband. When your husband is a winner, then you are a winner also. Romans 8:31 asks, if God be for us, who can be against us? When the victor is our Captain, it means that we have also won.

The Bible tells us that He has a name known only to Himself (Revelation 19:12-13). The Jewish name of God is Yahweh. This name was so sacred to the Jews that they did not even pronounce it. They said that the name was too holy for them to pronounce. They instead used the name Adonai. In several places in the Bible people asked God about His name, for example when Jacob wrestled with God in Genesis 32:29. Jacob asked God His name and He did not tell him. We are blessed today that we know one of His names, Jesus. We are also privileged to be allowed to call this name. At the name of Jesus, every knee should bow, on earth and even in Heaven.

However, there is another name known to Jesus only. There are several reasons why this may be so. Once you know the name of a person, you can command the person and order them to do certain things.

Your enemy, for example, can make you turn your face towards Him simply by calling your name. Probably, we will know God's hidden name when we get to Heaven. Meanwhile, we are satisfied with the name we know. At least, we know that whatever we ask in the Name of Jesus will be done.

THE SUPPER OF THE GREAT GOD

Revelation 19:15-21

> *And out of his mouth goeth a sharp sword, that with it he should smite the nations: and he shall rule them with a rod of iron: and he treadeth the winepress of the fierceness and wrath of Almighty God. And he hath on his vesture and on his thigh a name written, KING OF KINGS, AND LORD OF LORDS. And I saw an angel standing in the sun; and he cried with a loud voice, saying to all the fowls that fly in the midst of heaven, Come and gather yourselves together unto the supper of the great God; That ye may eat the flesh of kings, and the flesh of captains, and the flesh of mighty men, and the flesh of horses, and of them that sit on them, and the flesh of all men, both free and bond, both small and great. And I saw the beast, and the kings of the earth, and their armies, gathered together to make war against him that sat on the horse, and against his army. And the beast was taken, and with him the false prophet that wrought miracles before him, with which he deceived them that had received the mark of the beast, and them that worshipped his image. These both were cast alive into a lake of fire burning with brimstone. And the remnant were slain with the sword of him that sat upon the horse, which sword proceeded out of his mouth: and all the fowls were filled with their flesh.*

God is called the King of kings and the Lord of lords. This means He is the Controller of all the governments in the world both now and in the future. If you desire anything from any earthly government, first talk to the King of kings. If He approves, no government can disapprove.

On our way to Heaven on white horses, those on earth including the Antichrist and His army will see us and they will not want us to come down. God will at this time send an invitation to all the birds to come for a feast.

As John saw it, according to our Bible passage, out of the mouth of our Commander came a sword, which is nothing but the word of God to slay all the armies gathered. When they die the birds will eat their carcasses. God does not want us to start for the honeymoon by burying bodies so He will have arranged for the birds to clean up the place before we come.

When God is on your side, anybody who tries to block your way is going to pay with their life. If God says He wants to promote you and someone says it will not happen, then such a person has signed their death warrant.

Jesus is a wonderful friend but He is also a very dangerous enemy. If you are on His side, you should rejoice. If you are against Him, you had better change your mind. He is not someone that you should try to oppose.

Chapter 33

THE HONEYMOON

Revelation 20:1-4:

> *And I saw an angel come down from heaven, having the key of the bottomless pit and a great chain in his hand. And he laid hold on the dragon, that old serpent, which is the Devil, and Satan, and bound him a thousand years, And cast him into the bottomless pit, and shut him up, and set a seal upon him, that he should deceive the nations no more, till the thousand years should be fulfilled: and after that he must be loosed a little season. And I saw thrones, and they sat upon them, and judgment was given unto them: and I saw the souls of them that were beheaded for the witness of Jesus, and for the word of God, and which had not worshipped the beast, neither his image, neither had received his mark upon their foreheads or in their hands; and they lived and reigned with Christ a thousand years.*

BINDING OF SATAN

In verse 1 of the passage above we are introduced to an angel coming down from Heaven, with the key of the bottomless pit and also with a great chain in His hand. The angel laid hold on the Devil, who John refers to by four names – the Dragon, the Serpent, the Devil and Satan. The Devil, however, has several othes names. In Ephesians 2:2 he is called:

the prince of the power of the air, and *the spirit that now worketh in the children of disobedience:*

And, 2 Corinthians 4:4, he is referred to as:

the god of this world

Ephesians 6:11-12 also says:

Put on the whole armour of God, that ye may be able to stand against the wiles of the Devil. For we wrestle not against flesh and blood, but against principalities, against powers, against the rulers of the darkness of this world, against spiritual wickedness in high places.

Satan is called a liar, a murderer, a thief, the accuser of the brethren, and several other names.

Thank God that there is one Name that is above all the names of Satan. That Name is Jesus. If Satan calls himself a dragon, you can tell him that the Name of Jesus is above his name. If he says that he is the old serpent, just tell him that Jesus is above that name. The Name of Jesus is superior to the names of witches and wizards.

One interesting thing is that despite all the titles and names of Satan, when God decided to bind him, He sent just one angel. It was this angel that bound Satan for a thousand years. Some ask that since a spirit is something that you cannot hold, how can you bind Satan? To bind a spirit, you do not use a chain of iron but you use spiritual chains. 2 Peter 2:4 says:

> *For if God spared not the angels that sinned, but cast them down to hell, and delivered them into chains of darkness, to be reserved unto judgment......*

God preserved certain angels under chain in darkness. Also, Jude 6 says:

> *And the angels which kept not their first estate, but left their own habitation, he hath reserved in everlasting chains under darkness unto the judgment of the great day.*

What are the lessons to be learnt from the binding of Satan? First, God can stop Satan's evil works when He is ready to do so. Some people ask why Satan is still allowed to roam free. The answer is that God has a timetable. When the time comes to act, He will bind Satan.

Second, God does not have to send the armies of Heaven to deal with the Devil. One angel is sufficient for the job. If one angel is enough to deal with the Devil, easily one angel can deal with any demon. Third, demons are not a problem to God because Satan their captain is not. This is why you do not have to fear witches and wizards if you are a true child of God.

Satan will be chained for a thousand years and later be let loose for a season. Why set Satan loose again after binding him for such a long time? Firstly, it is God who determines those who are going to be free and those who are going to be bound. If I had my way, I would bind Satan today. God will bind him and then let him loose for a season, to show that He is to decide who is to be freed and who is to be bound. I thank God that He has decided that I will be free.

Secondly, God has His purposes and plans for every creature, including Satan. God did not make a mistake by creating Satan. Right now, Satan is doing a very useful job for God, although you may not agree with this. God has His purpose and plans for me. I did not come to this world by accident. God has His purpose and plans for you too. I pray that these will be revealed to you.

Thirdly, God needs darkness so as to reveal the beauty of light. Light will be meaningless when there is no darkness. Joy is meaningless unless you have tasted sorrow before. Holiday is meaningless to an unemployed person. God uses the Devil in order to reveal the goodness of Jesus Christ.

THE 1000-YEAR HONEYMOON

Revelation 20:4-6:

> *And I saw thrones, and they sat upon them, and judgment was given unto them: and I saw the souls of them that were beheaded for the witness of Jesus, and for the word of God, and which had not worshipped the beast, neither his image, neither had received his mark upon their foreheads, or in their hands; and they lived and reigned with Christ a thousand years. But the rest of the dead lived not again until the thousand years were finished. This is the first resurrection. Blessed and holy is he that hath part in the first resurrection: on such the second death hath no power, but they shall be priests of God and of Christ, and shall reign with him a thousand years.*

Here, the Bible refers to the first resurrection. A first resurreection implies that there must be a second resurrection. There will be two resurrections. In the first resurrection there is order. The first person to rise from the dead was Jesus Christ. You may not agree, for what of those that Elijah and Elisha raised from the dead. Even Jesus raised three people from the dead. When these people were raised up, they grew old and died again. The first person who rose never to die again is Jesus. He is alive for ever more.

After Him, there were a group of people called the firstfruit saints. These are the people referred to in Matthew 27:52-53:

> *And the graves were opened; and many bodies of the saints which slept arose. And came out of the graves after his resurrection, and went into the holy city, and appeared unto many.*

When Jesus rose from the dead, the graves opened and all the saints who had died in the Lord rose again. People saw them in the city of Jerusalem. When Jesus went to Heaven, He took these people with Him. They will never die.

Still to come are those of us who are to go with Him during the rapture. At that time, according to 1 Corinthians 15:51-54, we shall be changed:

Behold, I shew you a mystery; We shall not all sleep, but we shall all be changed, in a moment, in the twinkling of an eye, at the last trump: for the trumpet shall sound, and the dead shall be raised incorruptible, and we shall be changed. For this corruptible must put on incorruption, and this mortal must put on immortality. So when this corruptible shall have put on incorruption, and this mortal shall have put on immortality, then shall be brought to pass the saying that is written, Death is swallowed up in victory.

Also, 1 Thessalonians 4:16-18 says:

For the Lord himself shall descend from heaven with a shout, with the voice of the archangel, and with the trump of God: and the dead in Christ shall rise first: Then we which are alive and remain shall be caught up together with them in the clouds, to meet the Lord in the air: and so shall we ever be with the Lord. Wherefore comfort one another with these words.

When the trumpet shall sound, all those Christians who have died and buried, will rise. They will be part of the first resurrection. Those of us who are alive when He comes will find our bodies changed so that we can fly and thus meet the Lord in the air.

When someone dies. His soul and spirit goes to Paradise while his body stays wherever he is buried or wherever he died. When Jesus comes back, He will first go to Paradise to collect the people there who will stay with Him in the air. These people will then come down to the earth and pick up their

The Last Days

bodies wherever they were buried. As soon as the spirits and souls come into these bodies again, the original bodies will be transformed to come back again as a trinity. (God made us in His image:- a trinity of body, soul and spirit.)

When these people pick up their bodies, they will go back and meet Jesus in the air. Those of us who are alive and who need not go in search of our bodies will then be transformed and we will be able to meet Jesus in the air. If you are not born again, you will not hear the trumpet and your body will not be change.

Another group that will be involved in the first resurrection are those who die during the tribulation. They will come to Heaven when they die but they will not come to meet us in Paradise. They will go straight before the altar of God in Heaven. They will be the guests at the wedding of us: the bride and Jesus Christ.

When we arrive with Jesus, they will have to wait in Heaven for us to settle down on earth. They will come later to pick up their bodies and join us. After the first resurrection, there will be a gap of a thousand years when there will be no resurrections at all. The next resurrection will happen after the one thousand years and this is called the resurrection of the wicked. It is the second resurrection. The wicked ones will rise at the second resurrection and their bodies, souls and spirits will also come together. At the second death, however, their bodies will be separated from their souls and spirits.

If you belong to Jesus and you die before He comes, you will die only once – Hebrews 9:27. Those who do not belong to Jesus are going to die at least twice. I thank God that I belong to Jesus.

Earlier, we said that our bodies must be transformed for several reasons. One of the reasons is for us to be able to rise when Jesus comes.

Another reason is that there is a time of bliss that is coming, which will last a thousand years in the first instance, which our present bodies cannot take. God therefore must transform our present bodies so as to make them ready for this glorious prospect. Our present bodies are limited in the amount of enjoyment they can take.

Those who are not with us during these one thousand years will be in a place called little Hell. It is only those who endure to the end that will live for ever. Those who lay their hands on the plough and look back are not fit for the Kingdom of Heaven.

This period of one thousand years is usually referred to as the Millennium. This is the Kingdom for which Jesus taught His disciples to pray about, in the Lord's Prayer (Matthew 6:10; Luke 11:2). It is also the kingdom referred to in Daniel 2. King Nebuchadnezzar had a dream and saw an image with a head of gold, chest of silver and a body made of brass. Its feet were made of clay. Then an invisible hand took a stone and smashed the image into pieces.

Jesus is the Stone. He is the Rock of Ages. The Lord referred to this kingdom in Matthew 25:31-34:

> *When the Son of man shall come in his glory, and all the holy angels with him, then shall he sit upon the throne of his glory: And before him shall he gathered all nations: and he shall separate them one from another, as a shepherd divideth his sheep from the goats: And he shall set the sheep on his right hand, but the goats on the left. Then shall the King say unto them on his right hand, Come, ye blessed of my Father, inherit the kingdom prepared for you from the foundation of the world.*

What will this kingdom be like? What type of government will be in place there? Where will the headquarters of the Kingdom be located? How will authority be distributed? What will be its economic policy? What kind of animals will live in the kingdom? Will its citizens die? What will they eat and drink? We will make an effort to answer some of these questions.

The government of the Kingdom will not be a democracy but a theocracy. It will be a government of God for the people. In Luke 1:30-33, while talking about His Son, God revealed seven things that would happen:

> *And the angel said unto her, Fear not, Mary: for thou hast found favour with God. And, behold, thou shall conceive in thy womb, and bring forth a son, and shalt call his name JESUS. He shall be great, and shall be called the Son of the Highest: and the Lord God shall give unto him the throne of his father David: And he shall reign over the house of Jacob for ever; and of his kingdom there shall be no end.*

The angel used the words 'shall' or 'shalt' seven times in the above passage. Four of the seven things which he said shall happen have already happened. The other three have not been accomplished. The Lord God is yet to give Jesus the throne of His father, David. He is yet to reign over the house of Jacob forever. Also, the Kingdom that will last for ever is yet to be fully established.

Daniel saw this one thousand years coming, in Daniel 7:13 and 18:

> *I saw in the night visions, and, behold, one like the Son of man came with the clouds of heaven, and came to the Ancient of days, and they brought him near before him. But the saints of the most High shall take the kingdom, and possess the kingdom for ever, even forever and ever.*

Where will the headquarters of the Kingdom be? Jesus will be living on Mount Zion and the headquarters will be in Jerusalem. Isaiah 24:23 says:

> *Then the moon shall be confounded, and the sun ashamed, when the LORD of hosts shall reign in mount Zion, and in Jerusalem, and before his ancients gloriously.*

What of the manner of government? How will authority be shared? Jesus will reign over the world from Jerusalem. He will have his vice regents scattered all over the world to look after every nation. These will be from among those of us who come back to reign with Him.

What will determine how many people these individuals will rule over is already made clear to us in Luke 19:11-26. In the parable of the talents, the one who made five new talents from the original five given to him was given ten cities to rule over. The number of souls you win will determine the number of people that you will rule over. If you do not lead anyone to Christ, you will rule over nobody and instead, others will rule over you.

God has made it this way so that we can not accuse Him of favouritism. Winning souls is a task anybody can do. You do not have to be rich to win souls. Remember that it is not those that you win that are important but those who remain with Jesus. This is why follow-up is very crucial.

What will be the official religion of the government? Christianity, of course. Malachi 1:11 says:

> *For from the rising of the sun even unto the going down of the same my name shall be great among the Gentiles; and in every place incense shall be offered unto my name, and a pure offering: for my name shall be great among the heathen, saith the LORD of hosts.*

When the Kingdom comes, it is the Name of Jesus that will be glorified.

What will be the economic policy of the Kingdom? Joel 2:24-26 says:

> *And the floors shall be full of wheat, and the vats shall overflow with wine and oil. And I will restore to you the years that the locust hath eaten, the cankerworm, and the caterpillar, and the palmerworm, my great army which I sent among you. And ye shall eat in plenty, and be satisfied, and praise the name of the LORD your God, that hath dealt wondrously with you: and my people shall never be ashamed.*

The reaper and the sower will be overtaking each other. This is what is called prosperity. There will never be any devaluation of the currency because, you cannot devalue Jesus. The earth and its fullness belong to the Lord.

What about the animals of the Kingdom? Isaiah 11:6-9 says:

> *The wolf also shall dwell with the lamb, and the leopard shall lie down with the kid; and the calf and the young lion and the fatling together; and a little child shall lead them. And the cow and the bear shall feed; their young ones shall lie down together: and the lion shall eat straw like the ox. And the sucking child shall play on the hole of the asp, and the weaned child shall put his hand on the cockatrice' den. They shall not hurt nor destroy in all my holy mountain: for the earth shall be full of the knowledge of the LORD, as the waters cover the sea.*

It will just be like the Garden of Eden, before the fall. People will not kill each other. Animals will not kill each other. Children will play with snakes and they will not be bitten. The Devil, who encourages snakes to bite, would have been put in prison by then. The Bible tells us in Romans 8:19 that even the animals are waiting for this Kingdom:

> *For the earnest expectation of the creature waiteth for the manifestation of the sons of God.*

And also Romans 8:22:

> *For we know that the whole creation groaneth and travaileth in pain together until now.*

Will there be deaths at this time? Yes, there will be. Despite the terrible situation of the tribulation, there will still be some people who will still survive as we have learnt earlier. These people will be around when we come and they will be able to live for about one hundred years before they die. Their children will still be marrying and getting married. Those of us ruling over them will not marry or have children. We would have become immortal.

Chapter 34

THE JUDGEMENT OF THE GREAT WHITE THRONE

Revelation 20:7-10:

> *And when the thousand years are expired, Satan shall be loosed out of his prison, And shall go out to deceive the nations which are in the four quarters of the earth, Gog and Magog, to gather them together to battle: the number of whom is as the sand of the sea. And they went up on the breadth of the earth, and compassed the camp of the saints about, and the beloved city: and fire came down from God out of heaven, and devoured them. And the Devil that deceived them was cast into the lake of fire and brimstone, where the beast and the false prophet are, and shall be tormented day and night for ever and ever.*

Before looking at the great white throne judgement, let us briefly ponder on the fact that after one thousand years of the reign of Christ, which will be period of absolute peace, Satan is released. As soon as he is released, he will go round the whole world telling all those who were not in the government of Christ to rise up against Jesus and all His saints. The amazing thing is that people respond to his call and surround the camp of the saints.

At this time the saints will have no weapons because there will have been peace for a thousand years. However, as soon as the army of Satan is gathered, fire will descend from Heaven and consume them all. Satan their leader is captured again and sent to his final prison house where he will be tortured forever.

Satan is to be let loose after a thousand years so as to prove certain points.

First, that man's problems is not the environment, the nature of government or the economy. The problem of man is in the heart. Some people blame the government and the economy when there is no peace. Good government or not, people who will steal will still steal. The problem comes from within. Matthew 15:19 says:

> *For out of the heart proceed evil thoughts, murders, adulteries, fornications, thefts, false witness, blasphemies.*

Some say that if only we all have a good education we will no longer sin or steal. They say that education will change all of us for the better. This is not necesarily true. Jeremiah 13:23 says:

> *Can the Ethiopian change his skin, or the leopard his spots? then may ye also do good, that are accustomed to do evil.*

We have lawyers who are thieves. We have doctors who become rich by encouraging abortion. There are engineers who indulge in fraud. Education is not the solution. The only way that anyone can begin to do the will of God is by believing on Jesus. The Bible says that if any man be in Christ, he is a new creature (2 Corinthians 5:17).

Second, the Devil can never repent. Satan will be imprisoned for a thousand years yet he will not repent. One would have expected that the suffering of those thousand years would make him repent and do no more evil. As soon as he is released he will continue in his enmity towards God and Jesus Christ.

There are some people too who must repent. Those who make a proffesion of faith and then who backslide belong to this group. They fail to bear fruits. Jesus said anyone that is associated with Him and fails to bear fruit would be cast off by His Father (John 15:1-2). If God tears you apart, nobody can put you together. Another group who need to repent, according to the scriptures (2 Chronicles 33), include those who had tasted the power of God and then became involved in occultism. If this happens to you then you are in grave danger.

Third, Satan is the one behind all wars. When Satan is out of the way there are no wars. As soon as Satan is freed, there will again be war. Never blame God for the wars in your life. If there is any war in your life, know that it is Satan who is behind it. Our God is the God of peace.

When Jesus sits on the throne for a thousand years, there will be peace. As soon as Satan came on the scene again, wars come. This will prove the point that Satan is the author of the war in your life. It becomes easier to fight when you know who is your enemy. Never believe anyone that tells you that God brought war into your life to teach you a lesson.

Fourth, the Devil uses human beings to achieve his purposes. As soon as Satan is released, he will move around recruiting human beings. There will always be people who will yield to the Devil. Satan normally destroys those he uses after he has achieved his goal. If Satan has offered you power and you accept it, you will end up destroying yourself. You should always remember the story of Judas Iscariot. If you allow the Devil to use you, he will destroy you.

Fifth, God always wins all wars. Satan may start the war but God emerges the victor. Because God always wins, if you are on His side, you will always win. If God is for you, who can be against you? God did not say there would be no wars for us to fight. He knows that the Devil will start many wars. The assurance is that if God is on our side, we will win all the time. Psalm 34:19 says:

Many are the afflictions of the righteous: but the LORD deliverth him out of them all.

THE JUDGEMENT

Revelation 20:11-15:

And I saw a great white throne, and him that sat on it, from whose face the earth and the heaven fled away; and there was found no place for them. And I saw the dead, small and great, stand before God; and the books were opened: and another book was opened, which is the book of life: and the dead were judged out of those things which were written in the books, according to their works. And the sea gave up the dead which were in it; and death and hell delivered up the dead which were in them: and they were judged every man according to their works. And death and hell were cast into the lake of fire. This is the second death. And whosoever was not found written in the book of life was cast into the lake of fire.

On the day of the judgement of the great white throne, both the small and the great will be gathered. Death and Hell will be cast into the lake of fire. This is the second death. In other words, the second death is the death that will kill death itself. There is one death now that kills human beings but there is another death coming to kill death. This death is waiting for those who fail to repent. The first death will kill them and the second death will also kill them. Thank God, I am born again. Neither the first nor the second deaths will have any effect on me.

Now let us look at this judgement that is called the White Throne Judgement. We will consider ten points.

1. This judgement deals with the wicked ones who rebel after the one thousand years of peace are finished. The Judgement seat of Christ is for those who made the rapture while the White Throne Judgement is for sinners who failed to repent.

The Last Days

2.   All those who appear before the judgement already stand been condemned. If you find yourself there, be sure that you are going to Hell. One may ask, if they were already going to Hell, why bring them to judgement again? The answer is that this judgement is only to determine the extent of punishment. It is to decide how hot the place where an individual will be put.

3. It is from the Book of Life that God will check whether the right people to be cast into the lake of fire will be sent there. This is explained to us in Revelation 20: 12 and 15. Nobody will go to Hell by error. God does not make mistakes but because the judgement will be very terrible. God will use this book to prove that no-one will end up there by error.

4. There are other books apart from the Book of Life and these books will contain the record of all the work that we have done. It is from these books that those who come before the judgement of the great white throne, will be judged. In Ecclesiastes 12:14 it is written:

For God shall bring every work into judgment, with every secret thing, whether it be good, or whether it be evil.

Every work that you do in secret is being recorded. It is better to do only those things of which God will approve. You cannot hide anything from God.

5. The blood of Jesus has wiped away all your evil deeds, the day you came to faith. The blood of Jesus cleanses from all sins.

6. The Judge on the White Throne is Jesus. John 5:22 says:

For the Father judgeth no man, but hath committed all judgment unto the Son.

Adherents of some other religions say that it is God the Father that will judge all of us. They say they do not need Jesus. They will be surprised on that day when they find out who will be on the judgement seat.

7. Those of us who belong to Jesus will not appear before the judgement. He will only judge all those who rejected Him. All those who reject Christ are in serious trouble.

8. Judgement was so terrible and the face of the Judge, so frightening that the Bible says the Heaven and the earth fled. Some ask how can Heaven fly away? Look at Isaiah 51:6:

Lift up your eyes to the heavens, and look upon the earth beneath: for the heavens shall vanish away like smoke, and the earth shall wax old like a garment, and they that dwell therein shall die in like manner: but my salvation shall be for ever, and my righteousness shall not be abolished.

Heaven and earth will vanish but those who are to be judged cannot run away.

9. The sea gave up the dead. This means that those who died in the sea, rose up from the waters. No matter where. you died, on this day of judgement, you will rise to face the judgement and die a second time.

10. Those whose names are written in the Book of Life will not have a part in the second death.

Revelation 3:5, says:

He that overcometh, the same shall be clothed in white raiment; and I will not blot out his name out of the book of life, but I will confess his name before my Father, and before his angels.

God has promised that He will not blot out the names of those who overcome. It is only those who persevere to the end that we shall call overcomers.

If you want to get to Heaven you must live a holy life because without holiness, no man shall see God. You must bear fruits or else the Father will tear you off. You must never look back no matter how fierce the attack by Satan. I have made up my mind that there is no going back for me.

What about you?

Chapter 35

THE NEW HEAVEN AND THE NEW EARTH

Revelation 21:1-8:

And I saw a new heaven and a new earth for the first heaven and the first earth were passed away; and there was no more sea. And I John saw the holy city, new Jerusalem, coming down from God out of heaven, prepared as a bride adorned for her husband. And I heard a great voice out of heaven saying, Behold the tabernacle of God is with men, and he will dwell with them, and they shall be his people, and God himself shall be with them, and be their God. And God shall wipe away all tears from their eyes; and there shall be no more death, neither sorrow, nor crying, neither shall there be any more pain for the former things are passed away. And he that sat upon the throne said, Behold, I make all things new. And he said unto me, Write for these words are true and faithful. And he said unto me, it is done. I am Alpha and Omega, the beginning and the end. I will give unto him that is a thirst of the fountain of the water of life freely. He that overcometh shall inherit all things; and I will be his God, and he shall be my son. But the fearful, and unbelieving, and the abominable, and murderers, and whoremongers, and sorcerers, and idolaters, and all liars, shall have their part in the lake which burneth with fire and brimstone: which is the second death.

GOD IS WILLING TO MAKE ALL THINGS NEW FOR US

Revelation 21 is one of the most beautiful chapters in the Bible because it tells us about where those of us on the Lord's side will go. It also tells us where those who side with the Devil will end up.

John said he saw a new Heaven and a new earth. The Bible is full of promises of God for new heavens and new earths. Here, John saw only one Heaven and one earth. God will create Heaven among heavens. There are many means that there are at least three heavens. The Bible also talks of God living in the Heaven of heavens (Deuteronomy 10:14). God is saying that this Heaven will be changed. He is going to, as it were, change the furniture of His house.

Where God dwells is already beautiful beyond any human description. Here God is saying that by the time we have been with Him for a certain period, He will refurnish His home and make it more beautiful still. I am thrilled that I will be there. I hope to see you there, in Jesus Name. Isaiah 65:17 says:

For, behold, I create new heavens and a new earth: and the former shall not be remembered, nor come into mind.

The beauty of the new heavens and new earth will erase every remembrance of the old ones.

What shall we be doing when we get there? Isaiah 66:22-23 gives a clue:

For as the new heavens and the new earth, which I will make, shall remain before me, saith the LORD, so shall your seed and your name remain. And it shall come to pass, that from one new moon to another,

> *and from one sabbath to another, shall all flesh come to worship before me, saith the LORD.*

We will be worshipping God forever in the New Jerusalem coming down from God, prepared as a bride for her husband.

There will be two Jerusalems. For everything that will be happening in Heaven, something parallel will be happening here on earth. Just as we are getting married to Jesus, those who are left behind will be married to the Antichrist.

The Bible makes it clear that everything on earth is a shadow of what is in Heaven. When God told Moses to make a tabernacle for Him, He showed him a tabernacle in Heaven, which he was to copy. Moses tried very hard but a copy will always be a copy. All the things on earth, no matter how beautiful they are, will just be like mere pictures when compared with things in Heaven.

Just as there is an earthly Jerusalem, there is a heavenly Jerusalem. Galatians 4:22-26:

> *For it is written, that Abraham had two sons, the one by a bondmaid, the other by a freewoman. But he who was of the bondwoman was born after the flesh; but he of the freewoman was by promise. Which things are an allegory for these are the two covenants; the one from the mount Sinai, which gendereth to bondage, which is Agar. For this Agar is mount Sinai in Arabia, and answereth to Jerusalem which now is, and is in bondage with her children. But Jerusalem which above is free, which is the mother of us all.*

God gave Abraham two sons. One was born of a slave while the other was born of a free woman. All those that are in the lineage of the slave constitute what we could call the earthly Jerusalem. All of us who are set free by Jesus belong to the heavenly Jerusalem.

Who will be the inhabitants of this heavenly Jerusalem? Hebrews 12:22-24 gives us a list:

> *But ye are, come unto mount Sion, and unto the city of the living God, the heavenly Jerusalem, and to an innumerable company of angels, To the general assembly and church of the firstborn, which are written in heaven, and to God the Judge of all, and to the spirits of just men made perfect, And to Jesus the mediator of the new covenant, and to the blood of sprinkling, that speaketh better things than that of Abel.*

The new Jerusalem is called the city of the living God. This means that God will be there. Jesus will also be there. The angels will be there too. Jesus is the firstborn of God and everyone that belongs to Him belongs to the firstborn church. Only those who belong to Jesus will live in the new Jerusalem.

There are several things to note from verses 3 and 4 of Revelation 21; Consider, the joy of having God in our midst! God is going to dwell among us. There will be a time when Jesus will never leave us again. God has always wanted to fellowship with us that is why He made us in His image. The Bible is full of passages where God said He wants to have continuous fellowship with us. Jeremiah 31:33 says:

> *But this shall be the covenant that I will make with the house of Israel; After those days, saith the LORD, I will put my law in their inward parts, and write it in their hearts; and will be their God, and they shall be my people.*

Also, Ezekiel 37:27:

> *My tabernacle also shall be with them: yea, I will be their God, and they shall be my people.*

When God comes to dwell with us, Isaiah 35:10 says that, there will be so much joy that it will be difficult to describe:

> *And the ransomed of the LORD shall return, and come to Zion with songs and everlasting joy upon their heads: they shall obtain joy and gladness, and sorrow and sighing shall flee away.*

There will be everlasting joy when God begins to dwell among His people.

At the time, it is not only the redeemed of the Lord that will be rejoicing. God will be rejoicing too. This is recorded in Isaiah 65:17-19:

For, behold, I create new heavens and a new earth: and the former shall not be remembered, nor come into mind. But be ye glad and rejoice for ever in that which I create for, behold, I create Jerusalem a rejoicing, and her people a joy. And I will rejoice in Jerusalem, and joy in my people: and the voice of weeping shall be no more heard in her, nor the voice of crying.

This day will soon come. Revelation 21:4 tells us that God will wipe away all tears from our eyes. There will be weeping in Heaven. Some will weep when they see their reward while some will weep for joy simply because they have made it to Heaven. God, however, will tell us not to weep. He will take out His handkerchief and wipe off our tears.

In Revelation 21:5, we meet the One on the throne who said He has made all things new. Isaiah 43:18-19 says:

Remember ye not the former things, neither consider the things of old. Behold, I will do a new thing; now it shall spring forth; shall ye not know it? I will even make a way in the wilderness, and rivers in the desert.

God is willing to give you a fresh start. It does not matter how terrible your past has been, God is able to make everything new for you.

However, before God makes everything new for you, He must make you new. God is not going to change your circumstances until He has changed you. If you change, your circumstances will change. Let God change you. You must change or else your old self will destroy the new things that God could do for you.

THE ALPHA AND OMEGA

In Revelation 21:6. God said that He is Alpha and Omega. God is the beginning and the end. He knows you from the day you were born to the day you will die. He knows all the problems that you are facing. He even knows when the problems started. There is no problem that is outside of God's comprehension. God knows the foundation of all the mountains in your life and He can remove them.

In Revelation 21:7 God said that he that overcomes shall inherit all things. What does it mean to be an overcomer? Many of us think that once we become Christians, there are no more battles to fight. How can you be an overcomer without fighting battles? God did not say that there would be no battles to fight. What He said is that we shall win all the battles. There will always be examinations so that there will be promotions. There is joy in overcoming. When you overcome, you will

have a glorious testimony.

How can we inherit all things? Let us read Romans 8:16-7:

The Spirit itself beareth witness with our spirit, that we are the children of God: And if children, then heirs; heirs of God, and joint-heirs with Christ; if so be that we suffer with him, that we may be also glorified together.

There are two kinds of heirs. There are joint heirs and separate heirs. If a man had four houses and four children before he died, if the four houses were given one each to the four children, they would be separate heirs. If the four houses are jointly given to the four children, then they would be joint heirs. Everything that God has belongs to Jesus. Everything that belongs to Jesus belongs to us. We shall inherit all things.

Revelation 21:8 says that evildoers will be cast into the lake of fire. This is the second death. There are some people who will never be in the New Jerusalem. These are the fearful, the unbelieving and the abominable.

The Last Days

Others are the murderers, including those who kill with the pen and tongue, and whoremongers. Idolaters and liars also will not be in the New Jerusalem.

It is interesting to note that top on the least is the fearful. Unless God does something about many of us, we will qualify to be among the fearful. There are many fearful Christians. This is enough to disqualify us. Faith assures us that God is the Almighty and that He will win. Fear tells us that the Devil is the almighty and that he will win. There cannot be a greater insult to the Almighty God than fear.

Next are the unbelieving. These are those who believe with their mouths only. They proclaim God with their mouths and deny Him by their actions. Third are the abominable. They are the homosexuals and similar people. The next group are the murderers who kill with their tongues, pens and guns. Also included are whoremongers, adulterers and fornicators.

Idolaters are those who worship anything else apart from God. This could be money, status, other men, possession or power. We also have liars on the list. There are several types of lies – black lies and white lies – for example in God's eyes, this makes no difference. All liars will go to Hell, no matter the type or colour of the lie. I pray that you do not go to Hell.

Chapter 36

THE NEW JERUSALEM

Revelation 21:9-17:

And there came unto me one of the seven angels which had the seven vials full of the seven last plagues, and talked with me, saying, Come hither, I will shew thee the bride, the Lamb's wife. And he carried me away in the spirit to a great and high mountain, and showed me that great city, the holy Jerusalem, descending out of heaven from God, Having the glory of God: and her light was like unto a stone most precious, even like a Jasper stone, clear as crystal; And had a wall great and high, and had twelve gates, and at the gates twelve angels, and names written thereon, which are the names of the twelve tribes of the children of Israel: On the east three gates; on the north three gates; on the south three gates; and on the west three gates. And the wall of the city had twelve foundations, and in them the names of the twelve apostles of the Lamb. And he that talked with me had a golden reed to measure the city, and the gates thereof. And the wall thereof and the city lieth foursquare, and the length is as large as the breadth: and he measured the city with the reed, twelve thousand furlongs. The length and the breadth and the height of it are equal. And he measured the wall thereof, an hundred and forty and four cubits, according to the measure of a man, that is, of the angel.

THE GOD OF THE NEW AND OLD TESTAMENT

John had been telling us about the New Jerusalem. He saw the holy city come down from God, out of Heaven, prepared as a bride for her husband. All of a sudden, one of the angels who had the seven vials called on him to see the bride. He was taken in the spirit to a very high mountain and he saw a city descend. He described the city to us. The city is the New Jerusalem.

The city radiated the glory of God, which is described as like a precious stone. It had twelve gates with an angel at each gate. We can quickly learn something from here. Nobody will get to Heaven by accident. Nobody will be able to sneak in. The angels are there waiting to check whether you are qualified to enter or not.

These twelve gates are divided into four: three to the east, three to the west, three to the north and three to the south. On the gates are written names, which are the names of the twelve tribes of Israel. The city had twelve foundations and each one had the name of an apostle on it.

The city had a large measurement. There were no lights needed because the beauty of God supplied light. How can the presence of God light up a city? In God: 1 Timothy 6:16 tells us that the King of kings dwells in a light which no man can approach.

Wherever He goes, the light goes with Him. When He dwells in a city, His glory fills the city. We will be able to approach this light on that day, by this time we would have been transformed. If we went in our present form the light would destroy us. With our glorious bodies, however, we also would be shining.

With the city having the names of saints and the apostles of old, it means that God will bring the Old Testament and the New Testament together in His city. This is to prove that the God of the Old Testament is also the God of the New Testament. The implications here are obvious.

It means that God can do what He did in the Old Testament even today. He healed in the Old Testament and He is still healing today; he raised the dead in the Old Testament and He can still raise the dead now. The God of Elijah is our God too. It also means that old and new testmament saints alike are saved by the blood of Jesus.

Three of the twelve gates faced the east. Some bible scholars believe that these are the gates for those who accepted Jesus early in their lives. They are the blessed people who did not suffer much before they met Jesus. As for the three gates that faced the west, scholars believe they are for those who accepted Jesus late in life. They are those who suffered Satan's worst attacks and almost died before they accepted Jesus.

There were three gates in the north. The north of the world is always very cold. Bible scholars say these are the gates for cold people like intellectuals who had to examine Jesus's teaching before they believed. The southern gates are believed to be for those who can dance and shout and for those who received Jesus through their emotions.

We are told that the city was a perfect cube. When Solomon built his temple, the place was called the Holy of Holies and the Oracle of God in it was built as a perfect cube. This is in 1 Kings 6:19:

> *And the oracle he prepared in the house within to set there the ark of the covenant of the LORD.*

Bible scholars say that the New Jerusalem will be the Holy of Holies of God. It will be where the Almighty God will dwell.

When the city was measured it was found to be 1,500 miles long. The ground covered by the city was 2.25 million square miles.

I believe that what God is trying to tell us is that there is room for anyone who wants to come into this city. Jesus said that in His Father's house there are many mansions (John 14:2). Many as these mansions are, there will be the question of substitution.

THERE IS NO NIGHT THERE

Revelation 21: 18-27:

> *And the building of the wall of it was of jasper: and the city was pure gold, like unto clear glass. And the foundations of the wall of the city were garnished with all manner of precious stones. The first foundation was jasper; the second, sapphire; the third, a chalcedony; the fourth, an emerald; The fifth, sardonyx; the sixth, sardius; the seventh, chrysolyte; the eighth, beryl; the ninth, a topaz; the tenth, a chrysoprasus; the eleventh, a jacinth; the twelfth, an amethyst. And the twelve gates were twelve pearls: every several gate was of one pearl: and the street of the city was pure gold, as it were transparent glass. And I saw no temple therein: for the Lord God Almighty and the Lamb are the temple of it. And the city had no need of the sun, neither of the moon, to shine in it: for the glory of God did lighten it, and the Lamb is the light thereof. And the nations of them which are saved shall walk in the light of it: and the kings of the earth do bring their glory and honour into it. And the gates of it shall not be shut at all by day: for there shall be no night there. And they shall bring the glory and honour of the nations into it. And there shall in no wise enter into it any thing that defileth, neither whatsoever worketh abomination, or maketh a lie: but they which are written in the Lamb's book of life.*

Here. John described the beauty of the city. There is the mention of twelve precious stones, types of which we may never see before we get to Heaven, Four of them are green in colour, four were blue and the other four were gold. One thing is obvious here. God went all out and used the best things to build His city. The dust of the city was made of gold.

The gates were made of pearls. In the olden days, the most precious of all stones was the pearl. A man was considered wealthy in those days if he could get just one big pearl. Matthew 13:45-46 says:

> Again, the kingdom of heaven is like unto a merchant man, seeking goodly pearls: Who, when he had found one pearl of great price, went and sold all that he had, and bought it.

The gate made of pearl is a symbol of unimaginable beauty and untold riches. This epitomises the beauty of the city. Our God is a God of beauty. Our God is beautiful.

If God can spend so much time and so much wealth in building a city, you can imagine the glory of those who will live in Heaven. The Bible says the gold in Heaven is so pure that it looks like transparent glass.

The Bible says there were no temples in the city. What do they need a temple for when God is there? It is not a building that makes a church. The important thing is whether God is there or not. If God is dwelling in you then you are the temple of God. 1 Corinthians 3:16 says:

> Know ye not that ye are the temple of God, and that the Spirit of God dwelleth in you?

We are told that all nations will come to the city. All nations will be represented in the city of God. When the Bible talks about all nations, it means a group of people who speak the same language. As far as God is concerned, language defines a nation. God wants you to go and tell people of your own language that there is a city waiting for them in Heaven and they must be represented. Several times, God had chosen people from different nations to carry the gospel to their people and they had failed Him. Invariably, God will cut such people off and then lift someone else up to reach that nation.

You cannot represent your nation in the city alone. God will not allow it. If God discovers that you are not witnessing to your people. He will send for someone else to do it and you will lose your mansion. I will not lose my mansion, in Jesus' Name.

In Daniel 7:13-14, Daniel said:

> *I saw in the night visions, and, behold, one like the Son of man came with the clouds of heaven, and came to the Ancient of days, and they brought him near before him. And there was given him dominion, and glory, and a kingdom, that all people, nations, and languages, should serve him: his dominion is an everlasting dominion, which shall not pass away, and his kingdom that which shall not be destroyed.*

All nations, all people and all languages are to serve Jesus in the city. I pray that you will be there. I pray that your relatives will be there too. We are told that there will be no nighttime in this city. There is a day to come that will never end. God will have plenty of time to review our lives. I pray that you will not weep on that day.

We are told that the gates of the city were never shut. This is because there were no thieves there. The Devil by now would have been securely imprisoned. There were no sinners there. There were no impurities there. The beauty of the city will not be spoiled by any impurity. Nothing that is unclean will be allowed into the city.

Chapter 37

SURELY, I COME QUICKLY

Revelation 22:1-21:

> And he shewed me a pure river of water of life; clear as crystal, proceeding out of the throne of God and of the Lamb. In the midst of the street of it, and on either side of the river, was there the tree of life, which have twelve manner of fruits, and yielded her fruit every month: and the leaves of the tree were for the healing of the nations. And there shall be no more curse: but the throne of God and of the Lamb shall be in it; and his servants shall serve him: And they shall see his face; and his name shall be in their foreheads. And there shall be no night there; and they need no candle, neither light of the sun; for the Lord God giveth them light: and they shall reign for ever and ever. And he said unto me, These sayings are faithful and true: and the Lord God of the holy prophets sent his angel to shew unto his servants the things which must shortly be done. Behold, I come quickly: blessed is he that keepeth the sayings of the prophecy of this book. And I John saw these things, and heard them. And when I had heard and seen, I fell down to worship

> before the feet of the angel which showed me these things. Then saith he unto me, See thou do it not: for I am thy fellow servant, and of thy brethren the prophets, and of them which keep the sayings of this book: worship God. And he saith unto me, Seal not the sayings of the prophecy of this book: for the time is at hand. He that is unjust, let him be unjust still: and he which is filthy, let him be filthy still: and he that is righteous, let him be righteous still: and he that is holy, let him be holy still. And, behold, I come quickly; and my reward is with me, to give every man according as his work shall be. I am Alpha and Omega, the beginning and the end, the first and the last. Blessed are they that do his commandments, that they may have right to the tree of life, and may enter in through the gates into the city. For without are dogs, and sorcerers, and whoremongers, and murderers, and idolaters, and whosoever loveth and maketh a lie. I Jesus have sent mine angel to testify unto you these things in the churches. I am the root and the offspring of David, and the bright and morning star. And the Spirit and the bride say, Come. And let him that heareth say, Come. And let him that is a thirst come. And whosoever will, let him take the water of life freely. For I testify unto every man that heareth the words of the prophecy of this book, If any man shall add unto these things, God shall add unto him the plagues that are written in this book: And if any man shall take away from the words of the book of this prophecy, God shall take away his part out of the book of life, and out of the holy city, and from the things which are written in this book. He which testifieth these things saith, Surely I come quickly. Amen. Even so, come, Lord Jesus. The grace of our Lord Jesus Christ be with you all. Amen.

Right in the centre of the New Jerusalem, John saw the throne of Heaven. Under the throne he saw a river which was as clear as crystal. This river contained the water of life. David testifies to this picture in Psalm 46:4-5:

> There is a river, the streams whereof shall make glad the city of God, the holy place of the tabernacles of the most High. God is in the midst of

her; she shall not be moved: God shall help her, and that right early.

In Joel 3:18, another prophet said something about this river:

And it shall come to pass in that day, that the mountains shall drop down new wine, and the hills shall flow with milk, and all the rivers of Juda shall flow with waters, and a fountain shall come forth of the house of the LORD, and shall water the valley of Shittim.

The Bible tells us that those who are really in contact with God will find that out of their bellies will flow rivers of living waters (John 7:38). The words that will come out of their mouths will bring healing to the sick, joy and comfort to the sorrowful.

On both sides of the river there were trees that brought forth new fruits every month. This means that we will have plenty to eat when we get there. There will be many varieties of fruit. The tree of life, mentioned in verse 2 is perhsps the one that Adam was told not to eat from in the Garden of Eden. Those of us who overcome will eat from the tree.

There will be no more curses in Heaven. Satan, the father of curses, would have been imprisoned. When you fully surrender your life to Jesus, any curse put on you will turn into a blessing. There are no more curses in my life and there will never be anymore. We do not have to wait till we get to Heaven before curses will be rendered of no effect in our lives. Also, the servant of the Lord shall serve Him. In the past, people came together mainly to worship God. The purpose of coming to the house of God is for nothing other than to worship God. Every other thing is secondary.

Why is it that the worship in Heaven is mentioned so frequently? In Revelation 22:4, we are told that we shall see His face. Nobody will see the face of God and fail to worship Him. When we reach Heaven, the promise that God made through Jesus 2,000 years ago will be fulfilled. Matthew 5:8 says:

Blessed are the pure in heart: for they shall see God.

We shall see God and live. Before, no one could see Him and live. In Exodus 33:20 and 23. God told Moses that no one could see Him and live. By the time we see God, certain things will be very different. First and foremost, our worship will be perfect. At present, we are just imagining what He looks like. When we see Him we will really know how to praise Him. Secondly, our consecration to God will be perfect. When we are in the presence of God, we will have time for nothing else. Our surrender to Him will be total. This will also make our worship more complete.

Thirdly, the sight of the Almighty God will engender true loyalty in us. Perfect submission to God produces perfect freedom. When you submit totally to God, the Devil will flee from you and you will have no one to fear. You will also discover that if you submit totally to God, you will lack nothing. The moment you submit to God, the kind of respect that is given to royalty becomes yours.

Revelation 21:5 says that we shall reign forever and ever. Who are we going to reign over in Heaven? We need to understand what we mean by reigning. A true king is the one who lacks nothing and who fears no one. He is also free to do whatever he wants to do whenever he wants to do it. This is why there are really no king on earth except those of us who are children of God. There is no king on earth who is free from fear. At very least, he will be afraid of death. We are not afraid of death.

I am looking forward to that time when I shall reign with Jesus for ever and ever. I believe that we can begin to reign as from now. Whatever remains in our earthly life can be added to the reign that will last forever. We are already kings, according to Revelation 1:5-6:

> *And from Jesus Christ, who is the faithful witness, and the first begotten of the dead, and the prince of the kings of the earth. Unto him that loved us, and washed us from our sins in his own blood and hath made us kings and priests unto God and his Father; to him be glory and dominion for ever and ever. Amen.*

If we are already kings then we should begin to reign. The Bible says that we can rule even by decree now, according to Job 22:28:

> *Thou shalt also decree a thing, and it shall be established unto thee: and the light shall shine upon thy ways.*

Furthermore, we can bind and loose even right now. We can forbid whatever we do not want and allow whatever, we want. Matthew 16:19 says:

> *And I will give unto thee the keys of the kingdom of heaven: and whatsoever thou shall bind on earth shall be bound in heaven: and whatsoever thou shalt loose on earth shall he loosed in heaven.*

Moreover, we can ask for absolutely anything and be sure of receiving it, according to John 14:14:

> *If ye shall ask any thing in my name, I will do it.*

We can also be very wealthy, even now. According to the promises of God, we can have gold and silver in such abundance that we will gather it like dust, according to Job 22:24-25:

> *Then shalt thou lay up gold as dust, and the gold of Ophir as the stones of the brooks. Yea, the Almighty shall be thy defence, and thou shalt have plenty of silver.*

There are five conditions; which we have to satisfy if we are to reign now. Firstly, we have to submit to the King of kings, because it is His authority that will make us kings. Job 22:21 says:

> *Acquaint now thyself with him, and be at peace: thereby good shall come unto thee.*

Secondly, we must be willing to be ruled by His laws. Job 22:22:

> *Receive, I pray thee, the law from his mouth, and lay up his words in thine heart.*

Thirdly, if you know that you are a backslider, you must return quickly to Him, in the assurance that He will receive you. Job 22:23:

If thou return to the Almighty, thou shalt be built up, thou shalt put away iniquity far from thy tabernacles.

Lastly, never make a vow without redeeming it. Job 22:27 says:

Thou shalt make thy prayer unto him, and he shall hear thee, and thou shalt pay thy vows.

Jesus is coming soon. When John saw this vision, he was told not to seal the book because what he saw was going to happen soon. In Daniel 8:26. Daniel saw what was going to happen:

And the vision of the evening and the morning which was told is true: wherefore shut thou up the vision; for it shall be for many days.

Daniel was told that having seen all that would happen, he should not tell anyone yet because it was not going to happen in his time. It would still be many days to come. During the time of Daniel, Jesus had not even come for the first time. In our case, not only has He come the first time but He is coming back very soon. There are many proofs to show that He will soon come. We hear of wars and rumours of wars every day. Floods and earthquakes occur frequently now.

The Bible goes on to tell us those who will enter the New Jerusalem and those who will not. They are called sons and dogs respectively. These are the two classifications of people, as far as God is concerned. Those who are sons must believe on Christ and His sacrificial death, according to John 1:11-12:

He came unto his own, and his own received him not. But as many as received him, to them gave he power to become the sons of God, even to them that believe on his name:

Those who believe must wash their robes in the blood. That is, they must surrender their whole lives to Christ, their Saviour and Lord, for cleansing.

This shows us clearly that all those who believe that they can make it to Heaven through their own good works will not be able to enter. It is only the blood of Jesus that cleanses.

The dogs are those who have rejected Jesus according to John 3:18:

> *He that believeth on him is not condemned: but he that believeth not is condemned already, because he hath not believed in the name of the only begotten Son of God.*

There is another group of people that are called dogs. Proverbs 26:11 says:

> *As a dog returneth to his vomit, so a fool returneth to his folly.*

Also 2 Peter 2:20-22 says:

> *For if after they have escaped the pollutions of the world through the knowledge of the Lord and Saviour Jesus Christ, they are again entangled therein, and overcome, the latter end is worse with them than the beginning. For it had been better for them not to have known the way of righteousness, than, after they have known it, to turn from the holy commandment delivered unto them. But it is happened unto them according to the true proverb, The dog is turned to his own vomit again; and the sow that was washed to her wallowing in the mire.*

Who are these people? They are those who have backslidden. In Deuteronomy 23:18. we discover that 'dog' is the Old Testament term for a male prostitute:

> *Thou shall not bring the hire of a whore, or the price of a dog, into the house of the LORD thy God for any vow: for even both these are abomination unto the LORD thy God.*

Another qualification of those who can be called dogs is that they are liars. In Revelation 22:16, Jesus called Himself some names. He is the Root and Offspring of David. We know that Jesus is often called the Son of David. Isaiah 11:1:

And there shall come forth a rod out of the stem of Jesse, and a branch shall grow out of his roots.

Jesus is the Father of David and at the same time He is the Son of David, according to Matthew 1:1:

He also called Himself the Bright and Morning Star. This had been prophesied in Numbers 24:17:

I shall see him, but not now: I shall behold him, but not nigh: there shall come a Star out of Jacob, and a Sceptre shall rise but of Israel, and shall smite the corners of Moab, and destroy all the children of Sheth.

Then comes the great invitation in Revelation 22:17. Jesus is still calling people to come to Him. The bride symbolises born again Christians. The Bible is making it clear here that if you do not invite people to come to Jesus, you are none of His bride. Many of us have never invited people to come and worship Jesus with us. Please search yourself to know whether you are part of the bride of Jesus or not. John 15:16 tells us clearly why God has chosen us:

Ye have not chosen me, but I have chosen you, and ordained you, that ye should go and bring forth fruit, and that your fruit should remain: that whatsoever ye shall ask of the Father in my name, he may give it you.

All Christians are called to be missionaries. Our priority is to be a witness. If you have not been witnessing, you are a dog.

In Revelation 22:18 we have a note of warning. If anybody adds to what is in the book of prophecy, the judgement that we have been considering will fall on them. There are many churches today that add to the Bible. This is asking for trouble.

If anybody subtracts from the Bible, their name will be removed from the Book of Life and out of the holy city. Some people believe that the only part of the Bible that is true is the Book of Revelation. If you agree with them, then you are calling for your name to be blotted out of the Book of Life.

In Revelation 22:7,12 and 20, Jesus tells us that He is coming soon. He does not indulge in vain repitition. If Jesus keeps on repeating Himself, it means that you should watch out. The Lord is surely coming soon. All the signs point towards this fact.

In Revelation 22:20, some people said, 'Amen. Even so, come. Lord Jesus'. It is only those who are ready that can make this statement. Some do not want Him to come now. They have too many worldly preoccupations. There are, however, a few who are happy and eager to see Jesus come back.

2 Corinthians 12:9 says there is something interesting which relates to the last verse of the Bible:

> *And he said unto me, My grace is sufficient for thee: for my strength is made perfect in weakness. Most gladly therefore will I rather glory in my infirmities, that the power of Christ may rest upon me.*

Until Christ comes, His grace will be sufficient for us. It thrills me that the grace of God is mentioned in the last verse in the Bible. It is by His grace that we are saved. It is by His grace that we are kept. It is grace that has brought us this far. It is grace that will take us home. We will get there in the Name of Jesus Christ.

Other Books By The Author

1. The Bread of Life
2. Love not the World
3. Moses, Man of Destiny
4. Candidate for a Miracle
5. Victory: The Decision Is Yours
6. The End Time Army
7. Austerity to Prosperity
8. The Excellent Christian
9. The Child of Destiny
10. Behold He Cometh
11. Journey to Marriage
12. Jesus, Lord of the Universe
13. Prayer
14. Spiritual Warfare
15. Divine Healing
16. I Know Who I Am
17. The Last Days (Revelation)
18. Blessing and Curses
19. The God of Compassion
20. Walking with God
21. The Victorious Army
22. The Vine and the Branches
23. In His Presence
24. Dominion, Crowns and Scepter
25. Tree by the Riverside
26. The Swimming Axe Head
27. Joseph
28. Total Sanctification
29. Help from Above
30. The Lord Is My Shepherd

31. The Hiding Place
32. Spiritual Gifts
33. Arresting the Arrester
34. God Has a Purpose for your Life
35. Heaven
36. The Ten Virgins
37. The Gift of Love
38. That I May Know Him
39. The Sorrows of a Backslider
40. The Last Days of Elisha
41. David 1 and 2
42. The Siege is Over
43. Holiness (Part 1-10)
44. Pray Without Ceasing
45. The King of Kings
46. The Bride of The Lamb
47. To Obey is Better than Sacrifice
48. The Tale of Three Women
49. God The Holy Spirit
50. The Making of a Divine Champion
51. My Closest Friend
52. The Stronger Man
53. New Era
54. Heaven in your Home
55. Let The Fire Fall
56. Uncommon Greatness
57. Open Doors to Fruitfulness
58. The Blessed One
59. Possessing Your Possession
60. Open Doors
61. Ultimate Financial Breakthrough
62. Divine Encounter

63. Master Key
64. Showers of Blessing
65. The Awesome God
66. 65 Keys to Prosperity
67. Your Tomorrow will be Alright
68. When You Need a Miracle
69. Turning Point
70. Bible Companion
71. The Last Day
72. Avenge Me of my Adversaries
73. The Holy Spirit In The Life of Peter
74. Sermon of Blessing
75. Sermon of The Holy Ghost Service
76. The Almighty
77. Holy Spirit in the Life Of Elijah
78. The Hiding Place
79. Total Sanctification
80. The Ultimate Breakthrough
81. Help from Above
82. The Water and The Fire
83. Divine Relationship
84. Our Dominion Crown
85. God Can Change Your Song
86. Child of Destiny
87. The Crucified Life
88. Follow-Up in Evangelism
89. A Handbook on Personal Evangelism
90. Time of Favour
91. Marriage that brings down God's Glory
92. In the Footsteps of Jesus
93. Breakthrough Prayers for Leaders
94. Divine Collisions

The Last Days

95. Healing Meal
96. Essential of Prayer
97. Open Heavens Volume 1 – 9
98. Heaven on the Move
99. Flame of Fire
100. Ki Emi Ki O Le Mo